THE
GROWING
OF YOU

MICHAEL D. FLUKER

The Growing of You by Michael D. Fluker
Published by Rhapsody Publications

Copyright © 2014 by Michael D. Fluker
All Rights Reserved Printed in the United States of America.
First Edition

Cover design by Zena Designs Studio, LLC, Sarasota, Florida

This book or parts thereof may not be reproduced in any form, stored in a retrieval system or transmitted in any form by any means electronic, mechanical, photocopy, recording or otherwise without prior written permission of the publisher except in the case of brief quotations embodied in critical articles and reviews or as provided by United States of America copyright law.

For information regarding permissions, please write to:
Rhapsody Publications, Inc.
Post Office Box 991
Tallevast, FL 34270

This publication is designed to provide accurate, authoritative information in regard to the subject matter covered. It is sold with the understanding that the publisher is not engaged in rendering financial, legal, investment, accounting or other professional services. The author and publisher cannot be held responsible for any loss incurred as a result of the application of any of the information in this publication. If legal advice or other expert assistance is required, the services of a competent professional should be sought.

Scripture quotations marked by NIV are from the Holy Bible, New International Version. Copyright © 1973, 1978, 1984 by permission of Zondervan. All Rights Reserved.

Library of Congress Control Number: 2001012345

ISBN 9780972607223

I DEDICATE THIS BOOK IN LOVING MEMORY OF MY GRANDFATHER, RICHARD COOK.

Contents

Foreword by Dr. Marthenia 'Tina' Dupree

Preface

Acknowledgements

Introduction

Chapter 1 – The Parable of the Bags of Gold: 1
It Starts with You
Opposition to Your Ability
The Stewardship Model
Perceptions of Stewardship

Chapter 2 – Your Time is Valuable: 36
Excuses for Defeat
Where Does the Time Go?
Balancing Your Life: The Principles

Chapter 3 – Your Ability is Valuable: 62
Believe in Yourself Again
Gifts for Everyone
What You See is What You Get

Chapter 4 – The Power of One: Creation and Development   89
Creation Starts with You
Development Ends through You
Describe Your Talent

Chapter 5 – Your Money is Valuable: 114
Turning Your Sense into Dollars
Spend Yourself Out of Debt
To Have and To Share

Chapter 6 – Increase: 142
Make Sure What Goes Up Stays Up
Work is More Than Your Job

Chapter 7 – Management: 153
Mind over Money

Chapter 8 – Money Perceived is Money Received: 165
Walking the Budget Tightrope
The Money You See is The Money You Get

Chapter 9 – The Stewardship Model: 176
The End is The Beginning

Foreword

When was the last time you settled down in your favorite chair with a cup of your favorite hot beverage and enjoyed a really great book? Well it's time now. Michael D. Fluker has written just the book for you to enjoy.

I love to read and I read a lot of books. So when I knew that Michael had written **The Growing of You**, I was excited with great anticipation to sit down and begin reading his book. After the Introduction, curiosity set in for me to continue. I wanted to learn more from this author. What I enjoyed most was that I was able to connect with my life in the growing of myself. Isn't that what most readers want in a good book? To find out how their lives can be improved, or how to live a better life, or how to… whatever it is you may be searching for in your personal, professional or spiritual life. Michael uses a parable to validate meaning in your life. He gives great ideas for the reader to implement, and there is so much more that speaks directly into the reader's life. By doing this, he gives the reader a lot to consider in order to become more successful especially in how he uniquely uses the word "stewardship." He expands the meaning on what this word means in our daily life."

As you read this book there are many things to consider regarding your life that Michael discusses in the book. **The Growing of You** is a complete guide to self-discovery. You will find this book to be a positive influence on your life, now and in the future. I am thankful that I had the opportunity to read this excellent book.

Michael D. Fluker is a good friend and he has accomplished much in his life. He has not allowed failure as an option but focuses on success principles. He has reached his full potential and uses his experiences to help others obtain the same. I am delighted to contribute to this book by writing the Foreword.

Dr. Marthenia 'Tina' Dupree
President
Motivational Training Center LLC

Founder
Professional Speakers Network, Inc.

Preface

We live in an age where technological advancements have made the world smaller. We can use the Internet to access information from any source, any place, or we can use it to communicate with people from around the world. These technological advances have created opportunities for prosperity. With so many incredible inventions, I asked myself, "Why are people still living poor and unfulfilled lives?"

I wanted to know why some people absolutely love what they do – they greet each day with passion and power. While there are others who only exist – they live a life of mediocrity and rarely see the beauty of life. I asked that question more than 10 years ago, and after years of study and meditation, I found the answer, or rather the answer found me.

In 1995, I lost a promising job at a Fortune 500 company. My self-esteem was at an all-time low. Searching for a source of inspiration, I found it at the Westcoast Center for Human Development in Sarasota, a place I had never heard of, and through Dr. Henry L. Porter, a man I had never met. With only $100 in my pocket, I moved to Sarasota where my life began to take on new meaning.

After less than a month in the city, I got a job as an accounting clerk. Within two years, that job blossomed into a promotion as the Chief Financial Officer. I held that position for seven years before becoming a consultant and motivational speaker. I was the same person, but my thinking underwent a paradigm shift. I experienced a new dimension to living that enabled me to become more successful than I once thought. This new standard of living became a way of life to me through a principle called stewardship.

How did my life change from failure to success? The answer is simple. I was inspired by a story, or more specifically a parable, that taught me how to achieve success.

Acknowledgements

I thank God for giving me this opportunity to share with the world the gifts he gave me.

To the love of my life, my wife, Julie, I'm nothing without you, and everything with you. I know it wasn't easy spending so many late nights and early mornings apart, while I composed this book, but you persevered, and I appreciate and thank you for your love and support.

To my mother, Janette Graham, thank you for being a wise voice and reliable support in all that I do. To my grandmother, Georgia Cook, you said that I could do anything I put my mind to, and I still hear those words every day.

A heartfelt "thank you" goes out to my Pastor, Bishop Henry L. Porter, for your advice and guidance. Your wisdom continues to open doors.

I would like to thank all of my friends who contributed to this project. To Clara Cross, I appreciate your daily words of encouragement and guidance, making sure that I didn't become discouraged. To Derrek Gunnells, thanks for reaching out to help me during my time of need. To Reverend Henry L. Porter, II for helping me to see the possibilities again. To Dr. Tina Dupree for being an inspiration and writing my foreword. To Alechia Reese for building relationship bridges.

Thanks to my editor, Sheila Reed, for her editorial support.

Finally, to everyone else who supported me, thank you.

Introduction

A parable is a story that contains a lesson and provides wisdom or insight to the listener. Throughout the ages, parables have been used to provide clear and practical sense to real life scenarios.

We have learned lessons from stories such as "The Three Little Pigs," "The Emperor's New Clothes," and "The Tortoise and the Hare", but unlike these parables, which focus on one aspect of life (preparation, humility, and endurance respectively), the Parable of the Bags of Gold focuses on different aspects of success such as diligence, faithfulness, and courage.

In America, we have been taught that if we get an education and work hard, we can be successful. The Parable of the Bags of Gold took place in a time when public schools did not exist, and if you could not afford to hire a tutor, parables were an effective way to get an education. Hard work alone does not guarantee a life of success and affluence. You must have wisdom in order to know when to take advantage of opportunities. The Parable of the Bags of Gold highlights a great opportunity.

In ancient times, people of great wealth entrusted portions of their riches and property to stewards or servants; therefore, stewards were mandated to be faithful. The masters would then devote their time pursuing other matters important to them.

The primary role and obligation of the steward was to promote the interests of the master through loyalty or allegiance with the purpose of preserving, managing, increasing, and returning the master's property to him. One way a steward could achieve prosperity and success was to be faithful with the property entrusted to him. This is stewardship.

I view stewardship in an even broader context. We enter the world with no material possessions, and when we leave this life, we take nothing with us. Nothing we own is truly ours, therefore, it's our responsibility to faithfully use our time, talent, and money in whatever capacity we can.

Faithfulness in these areas will allow us to maximize our efforts in a manner that benefits our personal lives and the lives of others.

Each person has been given gifts and talents that, if properly developed, can make the world a better place. These gifts and talents come from a higher power, but it is our responsibility to nurture and sustain them.

What happens when a person fails to reach his or her potential? That person fails because:

- He or she lacks instructions.
- He decides to forego or ignore instruction.
- She allows outside forces to hinder her progress

In order to reach your potential, you need a tool that provides inspiration and instruction. **The Growing of You** is that tool.

The Growing of You will not help you to emulate others, but it will help transform you into who **you** were born to be. The process is comparable to the four developmental stages of a butterfly. Each stage of the "Growing of You" provides you with what is needed to bring about a higher form of **you**. From the corporate executive who wants to expand his business, or the homemaker who has dreams of becoming an entrepreneur, to the student who wants to be better than average, or the 9 a.m. to 5 p.m. worker in search of a better life, the "Growing of You" can help you reach your potential.

What makes **The Growing of You** inspirational to me, and to others who have embraced it, is that the principles discussed throughout this book can be used by *anyone,* at any point in life. **The Growing of You** is not a success plan or strategy, but its principles will help you succeed with the gifts and talents that **you** already possess.

Human nature often compels each of us to compare who we are to someone else. We look at those with money and believe that if we could walk in their shoes, we would be successful; or we believe that because we do not have talent that, we are not special. These fallacies are why so many people fail to reach their potential.

You are not like anyone else. You are unique, and **The Growing of You** will help you understand that it is the *application* of your time, talent, and money that will allow you to reach your full potential.

Over the years, I have seen people who did not have college degrees doubt their ability to succeed in life. Having a good education is beneficial, but your ability to reach your full potential is not based solely on your educational level. History is filled with stories of men and women who have succeeded without having academic credentials. If you are willing to take your skills, your passion, and your commitment to reach your full potential to the next level, **The Growing of You** is for you. Allow me to introduce you to this life-changing experience throughout the pages of this book.

Chapter 1
The Parable of the Bags of Gold

"Again, it will be like a man going on a journey, who called his servants and entrusted his wealth to them. To one he gave five bags of gold, to another two bags, and to another one bag, each according to his ability. Then he went on his journey. The man who had received five bags of gold went at once and put his money to work and gained five bags more. So also, the one with two bags of gold gained two more. But the man who had received one bag went off, dug a hole in the ground and hid his master's money. After a long time the master of those servants returned and settled accounts with them.

The man who had received five bags of gold brought the other five. 'Master,' he said, 'you entrusted me with five bags of gold. See, I have gained five more.' "His master replied, 'Well done, good and faithful servant! You have been faithful with a few things; I will put you in charge of many things. Come and share your master's happiness!' "The man with two bags of gold also came. 'Master,' he said, 'you entrusted me with two bags of gold; see, I have gained two more.' "His master replied, 'Well done, good and faithful servant! You have been faithful with a few things; I will put you in charge of many things. Come and share your master's happiness!' "Then the man who had received one bag of gold came. 'Master,' he said, 'I knew that you are a hard man, harvesting where you have not sown and gathering where you have not scattered seed. So I was afraid and went out and hid your gold in the ground.

Chapter 1 The Parable of the Bags of Gold

See, here is what belongs to you.' "His master replied, 'You wicked, lazy servant! So you knew that I harvest where I have not sown and gather where I have not scattered seed? Well then, you should have put my money on deposit with the bankers, so that when I returned I would have received it back with interest." 'Take the bag of gold from him and give it to the one who has ten bags. For whoever has will be given more, and they will have an abundance. Whoever does not have, even what they have will be taken from them. And throw that worthless servant outside, into the darkness, where there will be weeping and gnashing of teeth.' Matthew 25:14-30 NIV

The Parable of the Bags of Gold in Matthew 25:14-30 is the story of a man of considerable means who gave his three servants bags of gold according to their abilities. The first servant received five, the second two, and the third one. Each servant was responsible for the management and increase of his gold. The Master went on a long journey and had no contact with his servants. Two of the servants took the gold and, in faith, invested their gifts. The servant with five bags added five, the servant with two bags added two, but the servant with one bag dug a hole in the ground and hid his Master's money. When the Master returned, the servants gave him an account of their activities during his absence. Two of the servants found favor with the Master because they doubled his gift. The third servant did not use his gift. This angered the Master, who called him lazy and wicked. The Master took that servant's bag and gave it to the servant who had ten bags of gold.

As with most parables, the lessons they teach are relevant to our present day lives. As it was with the servants, we enter this world with nothing. Of course, some people are born into wealth, but this is not the norm. Everything we receive is given to us. In the course of time, most people discover their gifts and talents. Some people use their gifts to make the world a better place, while others fail to use their gifts to bring about significant change.

The Growing of You

The Growing of You gives direction and is the path to making a positive difference through:

- Power & Ability
- Potential
- Purpose

Power (time, talent, and money) paired with ability (level of proficiency) enables you to reach your potential (probability to produce) and will lead you to your purpose (why you exist).

This is the "bag of gold" that life gives you to make the world a better place. In order to maximize your power, reach your potential and fulfill your purpose, you must grow. Life is a process of trials and challenges that are necessary for you to develop these 12 characteristics needed to use your abilities to achieve your purpose, increase your wealth and expand your influence.

1. Acceptance (w/ Gratitude)
2. Responsibility
3. Accountability
4. Commitment
5. Diligence
6. Punctuality
7. Patience
8. Perseverance
9. Persistence
10. Generosity
11. Creativity
12. Frugality

We fail to develop the characteristics of success because we focus on the process, that results in complaining and murmuring about what happened during the trials and challenges, instead of focusing on the character development that brings us closer to success.

Chapter 1 The Parable of the Bags of Gold

The character traits of acceptance, responsibility, accountability, and commitment will be presented (in the It Starts with You section) while the remaining eight characteristics will be presented in the Time, Personal and Financial Stewardship sections.

It Starts with You

Acceptance

Acknowledge and accept your power. There is no one exactly like you. You have power, potential and a purpose. Unfortunately, some people complain about what they lack, or what others possess. In order to realize your own greatness you must accept yourself and what you have been given. Sadly, some people will not accept who they are, or what they have been given. This flawed thinking keeps them steeped in mediocrity.

There is more to you than you have seen, experienced and know about yourself. Your success demands that you change your thinking and accept your power. It starts with the appropriate response. That response is gratitude. My grandmother taught me gratitude when she said that I had to "clean my plate", meaning I had to eat *all* of my food because there were starving people who had no food. Another lesson she taught me was how to be grateful for my blessings and how to not focus on my problems because there was always someone else with more problems.

In the Parable of the Bags of Gold, the Master gave each steward bags of gold. There was a difference in the responses of the Good Stewards and the Lazy Steward. The Good Stewards responded with gratitude for the benefit of receiving their bags of gold. Gratitude is the attitude or emotion that acknowledges the benefit received. In gratitude, the Good Stewards were motivated to improve their relationship with the Master and trust along with faithfulness is the foundation of any relationship.

The Master's trust was evidence to the Good Stewards that although he was their Master, he desired to develop their relationship. The Good Stewards' faithfulness to his trust showed him that he could bring them into closer relations with him (Come and share your master's happiness).

The Lazy Steward responded with ingratitude. He viewed his bag of gold as an obligation to repay the Master which led to unfaithfulness to the Master's trust. Even if he misinterpreted the intent of the Master's gift, (Harvesting where I have not sown, and gathering where I have not scattered seed), he should have at least put the Master's money in a bank to earn interest.

It's been said that a grateful heart has room to receive more. The Master told his other servants to take the bag of gold from the Lazy Steward and give it to the Steward with ten bags of gold. The Master didn't give it to the steward with ten bags of gold solely because he earned the most. He gave the additional bag to him because he was given the most, and had the most to be grateful for.

Are you gaining more in your life from the use of your time, talent, and money? Ignoring your gifts does not absolve you of your responsibility to reach your potential.

Responsibility

Responsibility is the requirement to respond with appropriate action and/or activities that are in line with your ability, assignment given, instruction received, position held and resources of money and time available.

The Master gave the stewards resources, time, and positions that were in line with their ability to manage and increase money. The Good Stewards responded with the appropriate actions and activities.

Chapter 1 The Parable of the Bags of Gold

The Lazy Steward responded with inappropriate action and activities. After learning of the Lazy Steward's actions, the Master became angry. The Lazy Steward misinterpreted the Master's character as being difficult to relate to, requiring unreasonable demands on his ability, and wanting **more** from him than the Master gave him.

How you respond determines if you reach your potential. Potential is power and ability working to increase the probability of your power to produce. The Good Stewards accepted their responsibilities (took appropriate action) by using their powers (time, talent, and money) and abilities (what they're capable of doing with their powers) to double their gold (produce). Meanwhile, the Lazy Steward did not accept his responsibility (took inappropriate action) and failed to produce.

Why didn't the Lazy Steward produce?

What the Lazy Steward failed to realize was that his **perception** of the Master's character didn't change the fact that the Master's **position** was one of authority over him and because of that, the Lazy Steward was responsible to have **at least** put the Master's money in the bank so it could draw interest. It's wise to examine ourselves before we evaluate others. It's often the area in which we evaluate others, that proves to be the area that disqualifies us from advancing.

Your boss may have character flaws or possess less knowledge than you, but he is still in authority. People who desire promotions, but fail to receive promotions ignore this fact. I have been a supervisor and I have had employees who I grew fond of, recognized their potential, and encouraged them to reach it. However, those same employees failed to recognize my authority (by pursuing their own agenda), constantly questioned my authority (or my choice of those I delegated authority to) and did not follow my instructions. Their actions led to poor job performance that eventually cost them their jobs. They didn't follow the process. The successful employees didn't always agree with me, but they accepted and respected my authority.

The Growing of You

Your supervisor is not only evaluating how well you do your job, he is also evaluating how well you respect and follow authority. Your ability gets you the job, (and you are accountable for doing your job), but in order to be promoted into authority, you must exhibit excellent performance as well as understand, respect and follow those in authority. Ultimately, the Good Stewards were promoted for increasing the Master's bags of gold and for responding appropriately to his authority.

The Growing of You can help you learn how to embrace responsibility and prepare for accountability.

Accountability

Accountability is the requirement to report your actions and the results to someone who is in authority over you. The report can lead to consequences or reward. Accountability evaluates the effort or lack of effort made to reach your potential. The servants received the bags of gold based on their ability. The Master evaluated the stewards' actions <u>and the results they achieved</u>.

Let me explain. Each steward possessed the ability to double the number of bags they were given. The good stewards exercised PER formula for success. (**Power** from God+ **Effort** by man = **Results** in achievement) by going at once (implying that they went without delay), and putting their money to work (Effort by man).

Meanwhile, the lazy steward went off (implying that he went at his own leisure) and dug a hole in the ground and hid his master's money. The Lazy Steward failed to increase the bag of money and returned the original bag to the Master.

He relied on PAR (**Power** from God - **Absence** of effort by man= **Results** of loss and failure to achieve). Today, we define this as mediocrity. He gave no effort to develop his ability which resulted in failure to achieve and no increase. Burying a bag of gold in a hole didn't produce the effort necessary to increase.

Chapter 1 The Parable of the Bags of Gold

When the master returned and settled accounts with his servants, he evaluated their actions and results. Each of the good stewards doubled the master's money (five and two bags respectively). The lazy steward returned the original bag to the Master with an excuse for not investing his money. The Master believed that the Lazy Steward's fear of being held accountable should have prompted an appropriate response. That response was to deposit the money with the bankers, and receive interest.

Understand that you will be held accountable whether you want to be or not. The time, talent, and money you have been given is not for your exclusive use. When you live life expecting advancement or promotion without accountability, you deceive yourself. Possession and accountability go hand in hand. You can't have one without the other. The Lazy Steward's bag of gold was taken away and given to another who proved to be accountable with a few things qualifying him for promotion to be put over many things.

We all possess ability in varying degrees but what separates those with ability from those with ability who experience success is the effort made to develop it. The parable offers us wisdom on how to achieve success in whatever field we pursue as long as we follow the process and are willing to hold ourselves accountable. One day, your master will want an account of your work. There will be no excuse for your lack of action. We all have a purpose and must pursue it with commitment to reach that purpose.

Commitment

Commitment is your promise that you will work on your assignment no matter what for as long as it takes. Acceptance and commitment are connected. Acceptance acknowledges and accepts your power while commitment promotes and sustains appropriate action to develop that power. Together, commitment and acceptance create the perseverance necessary for success. Success is an attitude whose results manifest over time.

The Growing of You

Life presents situations and circumstances that might make your path to success harder to traverse, but perseverance (the willingness to continue working or responding based on your ability in spite of circumstances) will eventually give you the results you seek.

Commitment is important for growth, change, and reaching your potential. Possessing the tools for success is pointless without the commitment to use them in the face of opposition and distraction.

Opposition to Your Ability

In the Parable of the Bags of Gold, the Master entrusted three stewards with his gold. Two of the stewards invested the Master's gold and gained more, while the other steward buried his gold in the ground. Although they all received the same input from the Master, why did the Lazy Steward respond differently? He perceived the Master incorrectly.

"I knew you are a hard man, harvesting where you have not sown and gathering where you have not scattered seed. So I was afraid and went out and hid your gold in the ground. See, here is what belongs to you."

By his actions, the Master communicated faith in the stewards; however, the Lazy Steward's perception convinced him that the Master was a "hard man". His judgment was wrong and created resistance to the success the Master desired. If we are not careful, we can let our interpretation of our experiences and perceptions of our environment adversely influence our behavior. Misperceptions can make us fearful of our ability and cause us to hide the power given to us to help the world.

Keep in mind that what has happened in your life does not determine who you are, or who you are meant to be. The painful words you heard, the precious things you've lost; and likewise, the desired resources you lack do not define you. The power, potential, and purpose within you are proof of who you are.

Chapter 1 The Parable of the Bags of Gold

This means that your power, potential, and purpose are not subject to the limits of your environment or experience. Misperception of your environment and experience can keep you from maximizing your power, and exercising your ability to reach your potential and fulfill your purpose.

If you change your perception you will change your outcome. What can you do *now* that you're not currently doing? Is money an obstacle? Remember, broke may be the state you are in, but a blessing is who you are. It's true you may be broke, but you are not broken. You are more valuable than the money you possess. Have you forgotten who you are? Sure, the gainsayers had their say, but when will YOU let your power speak? Are you settling for a boring, predictable, and mundane life when you could amaze yourself by doing things you desire and are capable of doing?

In the context of stewardship, opposition can hinder you from exercising your power, reaching your potential and fulfilling your purpose. What is standing in your way?

Internal Opposition: Internal beliefs oppose you.

Envy: When someone else has something you want. Envy is a barrier to your greatness. Complaints about your lack and another person's possessions, cause you to ignore your power and potential.

Unwillingness to Forgive: The inability to forgive can lead to unnecessary pain, hurt, and sorrow all of which block your ability to move forward.

Circumstantial Opposition: External circumstances oppose you.

Lack of Money: You cannot see who you are for what you lack. When the absence of financial stability distracts you from your purpose, you neglect purpose and waste time trying to acquire money to survive. Instead, move forward with purpose and opportunities for money will come to meet your needs.

Lack of Opportunity: You have the tools to prosper, but your perception of the environment makes you feel ill-equipped to make progress.

Life of Ease: Your enjoyment of a carefree life becomes a barrier to your purpose.

People-Centered Opposition: People oppose your progress.

Comparison with Others: Other people seem to have more money, talent, time, and opportunity. When you compare yourself with others, you become blind to the money, talent, time, and opportunity that you possess. Stewardship gives you the wisdom to embrace your destiny and your purpose. When you compare yourself with someone else, those comparisons create barriers to your greatness and block your ability to use your gifts and talents to benefit others.

Programming: When you believe the negative comments or lies spoken about you, then you become subject to the things said about you. In addition, people oppose you by their actions. These actions do not support you, but instead threaten you in order to control you, or bring about a hidden agenda.

Company: You are the company you keep. The more time you spend around people with negative mindsets and unproductive lifestyles, the more susceptible you become to their ways.

In each type of opposition the central figure is YOU. The opposition must not define who you are.

It may seem that accepting opposition, from any level, is a legitimate way to protect yourself from failure and embarrassment, but nothing could be further from the truth. Opposition doesn't provide protection and is a barrier to your advancement. Allowing opposition to define who you are can be frustrating and is the single greatest threat to your power, potential, and purpose because:

Chapter 1 The Parable of the Bags of Gold

- It deceives you, and leads you to place limits on yourself.
- It contaminates your mind and makes you doubt your ability.
- It tricks you into believing that someone else's words and/or actions determine your success.

Opposition operates through the perception of lack, negativity, and comparisons, and is evidenced by statements like:

- I cannot continue because everything is blocking me.
- I'm not able to do it because I don't have what's needed.
- Because my family and friends say I can't do it, then I can't do it.

Opposition is a sign that you have great power, potential, and purpose. The path to purpose often goes through opposition. If you don't have the money, find it. If you don't have opportunity, create one. If you don't have the support of others, support yourself or find others who will. So many people give up at the first sign of opposition when in fact, this is the first checkpoint to your purpose. Overcome the tendency to give up at the first sign of opposition. The status quo is opposition's ally against you fulfilling your purpose. Will you surrender to opposition or fight to reach your potential? The vehicle by which we reach that potential is stewardship.

The Stewardship Model

Principles

I have observed that people whose lives are not "principle centered" — live "event-centered" lives. Event-centered living means that you allow events in your life to become your reality. The events create boundaries that limit your development and create a perception that your present state cannot or will not change. Your current situation may seem permanent, but it is not. Once you accept principled living as your standard for truth

The Growing of You

and reality, incredible things will happen. Opportunities that didn't exist or that were unavailable become available. You will literally be able to think and speak things into existence.

You might even say that your luck has changed, but luck has little bearing here. What has changed is that you are living in step with the objective reality of principles and not the subjective reality of your experience. You can learn from experience, but when you live by experience exclusive of objective principles opportunities for growth may pass you by. Let me share an example. Somewhere during the course of my upbringing, I asked my parents for something that I genuinely wanted. They said no to my request, which caused me a great deal of fear and reluctance to ask for other things. If I was hungry, and thought the answer would be no, I would not ask for food. If I needed money for a cause, I would not ask for assistance. This misperception evolved into my reality to protect myself from the disappointment of no. In 2004, I became the chairperson of a not-for-profit organization. During that time, a wealthy donor took an interest in the organization. For years, she made contributions to the organization that averaged $5,000 a year.

When I became the chairperson, the organization was at a crossroads. If we didn't receive $150,000 the organization's existence would be threatened. During that time I began to develop the Stewardship Model. I noticed that certain perceptions that I had grown up with, such as my reluctance to ask for help, had become barriers to my advancement. After some soul searching, I decided to ask the donor for a commitment of $150,000 over a three-year period. My board members thought I had taken leave of my senses. Nothing was further from the truth, but I had learned a valuable lesson. You cannot protect yourself with fear. What that means is, you cannot allow fear to cause you to remain the same in order to "protect" you from disappointment, failure or in this case the challenge of growth. It takes boldness to step beyond event-centered living. I did, and the donor said, yes. My actions changed the course of that organization forever.

Chapter 1 The Parable of the Bags of Gold

The Stewardship Model will help you live beyond event-driven boundaries. The model is based on nine life-changing principles that will help you shift your perception from event-driven to principle driven. These principles will expand your boundaries and transform your life in a positive manner. I believe that as it relates to stewardship, these principles establish the reality of success not limited to a person's race, nationality, age or gender.

These nine principles will help you maximize your time, talent, and money and establish success as your reality. Each principle will be presented in the corresponding sections related to the three types of stewardship.

- Diligence
- Punctuality
- Commitment
- Persistence
- Patience
- Perseverance
- Frugality
- Generosity
- Creativity

Insight

Fifteen years ago, during the time when I was suffering from great personal and financial loss, I moved back home to be close to my family and nurse my hurt. After a few months at home, I had an opportunity to move to a new city for a fresh start. It seemed risky, but I believed it was the best step for me. As I prepared to leave, my uncle, Leon expressed his concerns about my situation and said, "Michael, please don't leave. Your family is here, and we will help you get back on your feet, only stay here."

In all honesty, the thought had crossed my mind, but a real close friend said, "If you move to the new place and fail, then moving home is an option, but if you remain home in the face of this opportunity, then staying home is the only option." What great insight.

Insight is advice or wisdom on how to solve a problem or reach a goal without trial and error. Insight is the conduit between prosperity principles and action. The Stewardship Model presents six life-changing insights that help you reach your purpose and navigate life.

TIME STEWARDSHIP
- Efficiency
- Effectiveness

PERSONAL STEWARDSHIP
- Faithfulness
- Responsibility

FINANCIAL STEWARDSHIP
- Management
- Increase

My study of the Parable of the Bags of Gold, has led to the following conclusions based on the six stewardship insights.

- Each of us has been given a gift in line with our potential.

This pre-determined gift is with us throughout our lives. As with any free gift, it is vital that we learn to appreciate its value. Coveting or desiring another person's gift, devalues your unique gifts.

- Each of us is granted 24 hours in a day.

Chapter 1 The Parable of the Bags of Gold

Time is a powerful resource. The things that each person accomplishes with the same resource will be entirely different. Success in life is not doing everything in haste. The decision to use time efficiently and effectively for things that are important is what makes you successful.

- Each of us has a responsibility to manage our gifts and increase our abilities.

Gifts are treasures, but unlike material treasures, they cannot be stolen from us. They can, however, be stolen by us if we succumb to fear or selfishness and refuse to use what we have to help others. Instead of hiding our gifts, we should celebrate them and exercise them at every appropriate opportunity without shame or embarrassment.

- Each of us has the power to choose.

We can choose how we use our time, and whether or not we take advantage of opportunities and responsibilities. Those choices will bring results that are favorable or unfavorable.

- Each of us is given opportunities.

Anytime you find yourself envying the opportunities that someone else has, you will miss the greatness that resides in YOU. I once received an opportunity to speak in South Africa. As I battled self-doubt, I nearly declined the invitation because I began to compare myself to more well-known speakers and those with established track records. During my quiet time, these words of inspiration came to me, and continue to inspire me:

> **You will never realize the greatness you have until you go where greatness is needed.**

My gift made room for me, as your gift will make room for you.

Instruction

Instruction is direction that calls for action. The impartation of information is instruction. The Stewardship Model imparts information on how to use the time you are given, help you understand who you are, and guide your actions with the resources you possess. The nine areas of instruction will provide clear instruction that you need to achieve results.

TIME STEWARDSHIP

- Priorities
- Activities
- Significance

PERSONAL STEWARDSHIP

- Area of Gifting
- Belief System
- Development

FINANCIAL STEWARDSHIP

- Consumer
- Provider
- Producer

The Stewardship Model will inspire you to overcome opposition, empower you with principles for prosperity, provide insight for direction and introduce practical instruction for action. The results will be the prudent and profitable use of your time, talent, and money to reach your potential and fulfill your purpose.

Chapter 1 The Parable of the Bags of Gold

TIME STEWARDSHIP

- (Diligent, Punctual, Committed) **principle**
- (Efficiency, Effectiveness) **insight**
- (Priorities, Activities, Significance) **instruction**

PERSONAL STEWARDSHIP

- (Persistent, Patient, Perseverance) **principle**
- (Faithfulness, Responsibility) **insight**
- (Gifting, Belief System, Development) **instruction**

FINANCIAL STEWARDSHIP

- (Frugal, Generous, Creative) **principle**
- (Manage, Increase) **insight**
- (Consumer, Provider, Producer) **instruction**

Perceptions of Stewardship

We are creators. The ability or potential is innate within us. We create ideas, inventions, poverty, wealth, problems, solutions, and finally we create the world around us. The way we internalize our beliefs, interpret circumstances and relate with others shape how we view and experience the world. Because our perceptions are based on a subjective standard our perceptions and the realities behind them, often don't match. Stewardship is experienced through our perceptions.

The Good Stewards viewed the receipt of the bags of gold as an opportunity, while the Lazy Steward viewed the bags of gold as a burden. The Good Stewards gained more bags of gold and the Lazy Steward lost his bag of gold. Two different results formed by two different perceptions, one based on an objective standard and the other on a subjective standard, of the same reality.

The Growing of You

Today, our reality consists of time, talent and money, but how we view this reality contributes to our success or failure as stewards. In order for us to be successful, we need to understand our perceptions of those resources. The perceptions of stewardship offer insight into the tendencies commonly found in four types of stewards to observe how we utilize those resources.

Time

Successful stewards assign a monetary and personal value to all 24 hours of each day. They realize that in order to maximize their income, fulfill their purpose, overcome obstacles, enjoy their lives and contribute to the lives of others, they have to assign a value to their time.

To Good Stewards, time is a tool to maintain their lives and create things that don't exist. Good Stewards enjoy setting goals and accomplishing them. Because their time is so valuable they guard it diligently. They have no problem telling others no when people who don't value their own time try to infringe upon their available time. Delays and distractions are not options for them. Efficiency with results is their mantra. They scrutinize interruptions in relation to their overall goals. Although interruptions are reduced to a minimum, Good Stewards are flexible and can adapt to opportunities. They have lives filled with satisfaction because they manage their time effectively.

They take time to care for their bodies, nourish their spirits and souls, develop and maintain relationships, and educate their minds. Good stewardship is the balance between priorities, activities, and significance. Someone always benefits from the use of time, and proper time valuation determines who benefits, when and how much.

Personal Talent

The Good Steward has discovered that his life revolves around how best to maximize his talents and share them with others.

Chapter 1 The Parable of the Bags of Gold

The Good Steward accepts and embraces his purpose. He does not compare himself to others, because his uniqueness is evident. Belief is the vehicle by which he understands who he is, and what he has to offer.

The Good Steward believes that his talent can transform others. Connecting with the world through his gift is the key to making the world a better place. No matter how great the world is now around him, it will be better once he contributes his talent.

Financial

Good Stewards understand why it is necessary to manage and increase their money. They minimize expenses without sacrificing their needs and wants. Disciplined desires keep their expenses from expanding beyond their income. They meet their financial obligations, save, invest, and contribute to the lives of others. These individuals truly live the abundant life. For them, wealth begins with contentment and grows through wise investing. This mindset enables them to reap the benefits of wealth: to have options.

People who are content with managing and increasing their money are open to opportunities that contribute to the lives of others. Good Stewards live within their means with contentment and discretion. Their goal is to focus a portion of their energies toward increase. They can change their world by investing in others, owning a business, etc. This is the epitome of financial stewardship.

Efficient Steward

Time

Efficient Stewards place a greater value on accomplishing activities, instead of practicing their skills. Does this sound like you?

- I would love to learn _____, but I have responsibilities and just don't have the time.

- I will go back to school when my children are out of school, or in school.

- There are never enough hours in the day to get my to-do list done, let alone achieve my goals.

Because your life is activity-centered, you struggle to find time to practice the things that make you great. The Efficient Steward believes that everything else must be done first. This "all or nothing" mindset limits his ability to truly focus on things that matter. The Efficient Steward will never complete all his activities, because of how he perceives time: there will always be some activity that needs his attention.

Personal Talent

Five years ago, I received the inspiration to write this book. I knew my talent and what I had to offer. There was one problem, I didn't believe anyone else would be interested in my talent. For years, my journals were filled with points for my book. Hoarding my gift became a way of life because it made me feel secure.

Hoarding is the belief that your gift is not suitable for the world, only your immediate circle of family and friends. The Efficient Steward constantly works on *perfecting* his gift in lieu of *revealing* it to the world. Perfection is the Efficient Steward's mantra, but delay is often the result. In my case, everything needed to be aligned, the money to publish, the graphics designer, and the editor. The Efficient Steward doesn't want to face opposition and because of that, he won't move until all opposition has been removed. He perceives perfection as an event and not a process. The Efficient Steward believes that for every problem, a solution must be available before he can act. The Efficient Steward is conformed to the world instead of using his gift to change the world.

Chapter 1 The Parable of the Bags of Gold

Financial

One of my friends always says that he wants nothing more than to be able to pay his bills. His belief is that along with wealth comes a life of problems and greed. With that perception, he always looks for ways to spend less, but he is not open to opportunities to gain more. His perception of finances will prevent him from reaping the benefits of where his talent can take him: to prosperity.

Like many Efficient Stewards, my friend's financial focus can be summed up in the phrase: "maximizing the use of pennies, at the expense of creating dollars." In other words, the Efficient Steward will spend a tank of gas to save a dollar on an item across town.

Life doesn't remain the same, and neither does our financial status. If you devote too many resources toward acquiring "just enough," you create more problems than you solve. It is unwise to think that what we have now is what we will always have, and that what we have now -- will always be enough.

Effective Steward

Time

Effective Stewards are driven to get results. This drive helps them accomplish great things. However, the Effective Steward's use of time to practice and get things done is often at the expense of using time to accomplish other activities that together make for a rewarding life.

Do you find yourself making statements like these?

- Sleep is for people who don't _____.

- Why plan, something else always comes up, I would rather get things done.

- I spend so much time working to create a better life for _____, and they don't appreciate it.

Ironically, the things that the Effective Steward spends time on, creates results, but what he avoids spending time on, creates consequences. The consequences of improper nutrition and inadequate sleep are poor health. The consequences of avoiding people are broken relationships or no relationships. The Effective Steward accomplishes impressive results, but at a cost. For what shall it profit a man to gain the whole world only to lose his soul?

Personal Talent

The Effective Steward desires to impact the world. This desire is based on his endless dreams of greatness, but he has not discovered his talent. The Effective Steward allows obstacles to hinder his journey to self-discovery. These obstacles arise because the Effective Steward fails to plan. In his mind, actions and results are the only things that matter. More often than not, these obstacles arise from ineffective planning.

Lack of planning has its roots in the perception that action and results now, are all that matter. His desk is a mess, he can't find his keys. His car is dirty, but he is working on his dreams of greatness. Because the Effective Steward does not have a plan, obstacles prove to be effective hindrances to personal stewardship.

Financial

These stewards have the ability and desire to increase. Their downfall is the lack of financial management. They have no plan to manage what they create. One of my former clients possessed an uncanny ability to make money. Unfortunately, his lack of management skills caused him to pay his bills late and sometimes not at all. This resulted in him losing money to late fees.

Chapter 1 The Parable of the Bags of Gold

In addition, this prevents him from re-investing his money to earn more money. The financial lifestyle of Effective Stewards are unmanageable and without restraint. They believe they deserve to enjoy the fruits of their labor. They are correct, but their enjoyment knows no limit. They live above their means and are one emergency away from a financial disaster.

Lazy Steward-Time

To the Lazy Steward life is about avoiding purpose and potential in order to pursue relaxation and entertainment. The Lazy Steward is easily influenced by outside forces that end up controlling his time, talent, and money.

If you are not as successful as you would like to be, then examine how you use your time. A man who loves pleasure above all else--will be poor. There is a relationship between time and money. If you spend all your time at the movies, the movie industry gets rich. If you spend all of your time buying music, the music industry get rich. If you do not discover your talent or establish habits that lead to your success, then time is not your asset, it's your liability.

Personal Talent

The Lazy Steward allows distractions, obstacles, and failures to block him from using his gift. Opportunities mean nothing to him because he has no interest in discovering how he might impact the world. Studying, growing, and taking responsibility require too much work, and the Lazy Steward doesn't think he has anything to offer. His comfort is what matters most, not his contribution to the world.

The passage of time without fulfillment of his dream is "proof" that he is not good enough. The Lazy Steward believes that avoiding purpose is his purpose. Each time he avoids his purpose, it creates another barrier to using his gift to reach his true purpose.

Financial

The Lazy Steward is unable, or has no desire, to manage his money. He spends his money on the latest fad or must-have gadget and rarely shops for bargains. Want and desire are his financial managers. His mantra is *if you have money tomorrow, you are not enjoying today.* Outside forces dictate the Lazy Steward's inability to increase; therefore he looks for lucky breaks. Do you find yourself making statements like these:

- I'm just not lucky like_____
- It's not fair that I'm _____

The Lazy Steward does not trust anyone to help him manage his money, so he digs an even deeper hole filled with desperate attempts to increase his earnings. "Get rich quick" products and schemes endorsed by others —become the Lazy Steward's attempt at ending his financial death spiral.

Hindrances to Good Stewardship

After a long time the master of those servants returned and settled accounts with them. Then the man who had received the one talent came. 'Master,' he said, 'I knew that you are a hard man, harvesting where you have not sown and gathering where you have not scattered seed. So I was afraid and went out and hid your talent in the ground. See, here is what belongs to you.' Matthew 25:19, 24-25 NIV

The greatest hindrance to building stewardship is when we compare ourselves with others who possess greater gifts and a greater measure of money. We love to rank things and people. There are lists for billionaires, television shows, businesses, restaurants, chefs, and cars, etc. Rankings have their place, but not as tools for self-evaluation and comparison. Comparing your gifts to others can lead you to develop a perception that you lack what's necessary to succeed. If the steward who received

Chapter 1 The Parable of the Bags of Gold

two talents were to compare himself to the steward with five talents, their conversation might sound like this today:

I truly enjoy doing _____ and I'm pretty good at it, but I'm not as good as _____ therefore, I'm too embarrassed to exercise my gift to _____ or I wish that I had as much money as _____ then I would use my money to invest in or give to_____.

In today's society, an increasing number of people are trying to do and focus on more activities. Social networking, news feeds, cell phones, texting, email, and other gadgetry used to keep pace can lead to an overload of information.

When people try to do more and focus on everything, this draws their attention to multiple sources resulting in an increase in multi-tasking as a solution. The focus is no longer on one thing at one time, but on everything all the time. These attention grabbing devices dictate the pace of your life and trick you into believing that you have go with the flow resulting in no control over your time, talent, and money. For some, this may be true if you follow the world's P.A.C.E.

- **Powerless**
- **Avoidance**
- **Cares**
- **Expectations**

Powerless is the inability to produce an effect. The world does not encourage people to maximize their potential. Instead, the world deceives people into underestimating their value and into believing that they are unable to effect change. Left unchecked, you develop a sense of powerlessness, although you possess power. Using your power to grow no longer matters in your life — survival becomes the primary goal. This is the thought of the powerless.

Avoidance is the desire to bypass or keep away from something or someone. When you perceive yourself as powerless, it becomes easy to not use your gift. The gift that could help others, no longer matters to you. Fear becomes a catalyst to avoid responsibility.

Cares represent a troubled state of mind caused by the worries and anxieties of life. When you focus on your losses and the anxiety of lack, a type of psychosis develops where outside forces control your life. Cares wrap themselves around you like thorns and thistles. They choke your power, divert your attention, and leave you feeling like a victim – not a conqueror.

Expectations are to regard something as likely to happen. Expectations can affect your sight (vision) and undermine your sense of responsibility. When you focus on the expectations of others, fears of failure adds a level of performance anxiety not required by the opportunity or the responsibility. This can cause you to make decisions based on fear and anxiety in order to please others. There is hope. You can become a Good Steward by fulfilling the law of stewardship.

You shall reap what you sow.

Quite simply: whatever you plant, you will grow. If you plant orange seeds, those seeds will produce an orange tree. In like manner, if you sow unfaithfulness, you shall reap the consequences of that action. If you decide to sow Action, Increase, and Faithfulness you shall reap the benefits of success, rulership, and prosperity.

1. Act or Be Acted Upon
2. Faithfulness in Little, then Rulership in Much
3. Increase or Decrease

Act or Be Acted Upon

"Again, it will be like a man going on a journey, who called his servants and entrusted his wealth to them. To one he gave five

Chapter 1 The Parable of the Bags of Gold

bags of gold, to another two bags, and to another one bag, each according to his ability. Then he went on his journey. The man who had received five bags of gold <u>went at once and put his money to work</u> and gained five bags more. So also, the one with two bags of gold gained two more. But the man who had received one bag <u>went off, dug a hole in the ground and hid his master's money</u>. Matthew 25:14-18 NIV

Your actions and your perception of the actions others commit, can impact your life. It is important that you understand how actions lead to success. Taking action is the key to attraction. I define attraction as something brought to you by your action. I have talked to people who believe that simply desiring something will attract that desire to their lives. When they don't get what they want, they become disappointed. Simply wanting something is not enough. Your desires have to be strong enough to change your mindset and your actions. If your desire is to lose weight, you must be strong enough to change your diet and increase your physical activity. If you want to receive, you must ask; if you want to find, you must seek; and if you want a door opened, you must knock.

You may not control when or how a door opens, but one thing is certain, the door will not open if you don't knock. Success is tied to your actions. In general, people enjoy being acted upon, limiting their level of success. In other words, they enjoy being entertained or distracted by the actions of others to such a degree that it prevents them from taking action in their own lives. Distractions mean that the actions of others can hinder you from taking action.

Here's an example: Reality shows have promoted people with no talent into household names. The lives of these so-called "stars" are tracked day and night and are available for all to see. A byproduct of their accessibility has been a transfer of wealth from the hands of the many, to the hands of a few. Television, movies, music, social networking, and games (video and sports) are known distractions. The byproduct is that these actors, singers, social media moguls, and athletes are among the wealthiest people in the world.

If you fail to act, the things that come into your life are a by-product of the actions of others or your fear to act. Fear is a distraction. Most people prefer to wait until fear passes, but fear does not go away. Fear acts upon us and prevents us from doing what we desire. I learned this prior to writing the "Growing of You."

I had the idea for this book for five years before I began to write. But fear made me believe that no one would buy the book, that it would not help anyone; that the money needed for publishing would not be available. These doubts and fears acted upon me, delayed the completion of a book that I was clearly inspired to write. I wanted to solve these problems before I acted, but here's the thing -- waiting did not make my fears go away. In fact, I felt worse because I wasn't doing what I knew I was supposed to do.

Are there dreams and goals deep in your heart, that fears prevent you from pursuing?

Like the Lazy Steward, I buried my talents in the ground. But one day, I took action and began to write. Whenever I lacked assistance, I asked; if I needed information, I found it; and if a door closed, I knocked until it opened. Action became my response to obstacle. Had I chosen to respond like a Good Steward and began writing immediately, all those negative expectations would not have had an opportunity to exert their influence over me for five years. Fear caused me to delay being faithful to what I was inspired to do.

Increase or Decrease

After a long time the master of those servants returned and settled accounts with them. The man who had received five bags of gold brought the other five. 'Master,' he said, 'you entrusted me with five bags of gold. See, I have gained five more.' "The

Chapter 1 The Parable of the Bags of Gold

man with two bags of gold also came. 'Master,' he said, 'you entrusted me with two bags of gold; see, I have gained two more. "Then the man who had received one bag of gold came. 'Master,' he said, 'I knew that you are a hard man, harvesting where you have not sown and gathering where you have not scattered seed. So I was afraid and went out and hid your gold in the ground. See, here is what belongs to you? Well then, you should have put my money on deposit with the bankers, so that when I returned I would have received it back with interest.".' "Take the bag of gold from him and give it to the one who has ten bags. <u>For whoever has, will be given more, and they will have an abundance. Whoever does not have, even what they have will be taken from them.</u>" -- Matthew 25:19-20, 22, 24-25, 27-29

Related to the first law of Act or Be Acted Upon is the law of Increase or Decrease. The choice made to follow the first law results in the outcome of the second law. Action adds, while inaction subtracts. Action (savings, investing, planning, practicing, etc.) leads to increase and inaction leads to decrease, and eventually outside forces (taxes, opposition, trials, distractions, etc.) will take your time, talent, and money.

The world is in a state of change, and if you don't respond proactively, the world system will force itself on you. How many of you feel compelled to constantly check your email, text, voicemail, or social media accounts? You are being acted upon, leading to a decrease in time (productivity), and money (profitability) because you are distracted while your information is sold to the highest bidder.

Faithfulness in Little, Then Rulership in Much

"The man with two bags of gold also came. "Master,' he said, 'you entrusted me with two bags of gold; see, I have gained two more.' "His master replied, 'Well done, good and faithful servant! <u>You have been faithful with a few things; I will put you in charge of many things.</u> Come and share your master's happiness!'"-- Matthew 25:22-23

In the parable of the bags of gold, the Master gave each steward gold in proportion to his ability. The ultimate purpose for the stewards was to manage the bags of gold and return the bags to the master with an increase.

The Good Stewards went about using their abilities to increase their portion, and as a result, they increased themselves when the Master rewarded. Their stewardship led to rulership (over cities), which included ownership.

The third law of good stewardship is **Faithfulness in Little, then Rulership in Much.**

A strong sense of faithfulness and responsibility is essential for any ruler. This is part of a person's character and is best observed when charged with small matters. If a matter is entrusted into your hands, it must become important to you. Once you accept faithfulness in small matters, you prepare yourself for rulership over larger things.

I once had a conversation with a woman who had chronic financial trouble. She often spent her money on snack foods and other non-essential items. Unfortunately, she could not see how spending $2 or $5 here or there, impacted her financial situation. She was not faithful with small amounts of money and her spending habits showed she was unprepared for rulership over her money. I advised her to follow the three laws of good stewardship, with emphasis on the third law. Being faithful with a few dollars would position her to rule many dollars. Most people don't understand that how you handle a few dollars determines what you will do with many dollars. Wishing for much doesn't mean you are prepared to rule much. Take a few moments and Google "broke lottery winners" and read the stories of people who were given much, but weren't prepared to rule much.

Chapter 1 The Parable of the Bags of Gold

Summary:

Stewardship is the process that leads from ordinary to extraordinary through the management of your time, talent, and money. Power (in the form of time, talent, and money) paired with potential (probability of that power to produce) will lead you to your purpose (why you exist).

Opposition is the single greatest threat to your power, potential, and purpose because:

- It deceives you, and leads you to place limits on yourself.

- It contaminates your mind and distorts your thinking.

- It tricks you into believing that someone else's words and/or actions determine your success.

Walking in the world's pace (P.A.C.E.) is a hindrance to stewardship.

- Powerless
- Avoidance
- Cares
- Expectations

You shall reap what you sow. Although many of us live in urban areas, the principles of farming are applicable here. Whatever you plant, you will grow.

Establish Good Stewardship through three principles:

- Act or be acted upon
- Increase or Decrease
- Faithfulness in little, then rulership in much

The Growing of You

Reflect: There are three types of stewardship: Time, Personal and Financial. Contained within each type of stewardship are four types of stewards: Good Steward, Efficient Steward, Effective Steward and Lazy Steward. On the following page, read the questions and write the letter in the blank for the statement that best describes your personal stewardship style. Be honest, and be encouraged. By reading this book you have taken the first step to becoming a better steward.

1. Regarding my **time stewardship** style, I'm a _____.
   a. *Good Steward* because I manage my time and give priority to my mission, pursuits, and activities.
   b. *Efficient Steward* because accomplishing activities is more important to me than practicing my skill or maximizing my ability.
   c. *Effective Steward* because practicing my skill or ability is more important than getting things done.
   d. *Lazy Steward* because I let outside forces (entertainment and the desires of others) control my time.

2. Regarding my **personal stewardship** style, I'm a _____.
   a. *Good Steward* because I have discovered my talent and acknowledge my responsibility to develop and contribute it to the world.
   b. *Efficient Steward* because I have discovered my talent, but don't believe that anyone is interested in what I have to offer, therefore I hide my gift.
   c. *Effective Steward* because I have endless dreams of greatness and a desire to impact the world, but I have not discovered my talent because obstacles, distractions, and failures hinder me.
   d. *Lazy Steward* because I have no interest in discovering my talent.

Chapter 1 The Parable of the Bags of Gold

3. Regarding my **financial stewardship** style, I'm a _____.

   a. *Good Steward* because I manage my money through planning and wise spending, therefore I am able to increase my saving, giving, and investing.
   b. *Efficient Steward* because I manage money well; however, I fail to make plans to increase my money.
   c. *Effective Steward* because I have the ability and desire to increase my money, but I do not manage the increase.
   d. *Lazy Steward* because I do not manage my money. I have to "rob Peter to pay Paul", and constantly find myself with "not enough".

4. I want to learn how to improve my personal, time and financial stewardship because

   _____
   _____
   _____
   _____
   _____
   _____
   _____
   _____

In this introduction to stewardship, many of you have been challenged to assess the perceptions and values you place on your time, talent, and money. This assessment provides insight into the type of steward you are. It also shows how to improve

5% or .5/10 and how to ensure that your life is spent being productive and prosperous. Your present situation is a starting point. It is in no way a reflection of your complete self. The Stewardship Model will help you fulfill your purpose, overcome obstacles, enjoy your life, and contribute to the lives of others.

CHAPTER 2
Your Time is Valuable

Acknowledge – 24 hours per day
Accept responsibility – to get things done effectively
Affirm – to work efficiently
Act – as if each day was your last to build yourself and others in the world. (schedule, plan, goals)

> "Then the man who had received one bag of gold came. 'Master,' he said, 'I knew that you are a hard man, harvesting where you have not sown and gathering where you have not scattered seed. So I was afraid and went out and hid your gold in the ground. See, here is what belongs to you.' Matthew 25: 24-25 NIV

Excuses for Defeat

After making their report, the Good Stewards were rewarded by their master. The Lazy Steward made his report and it was not good. He presented his original bag of gold to the master. The Lazy Steward did not use his time to complete his task. He allowed fear to prompt him to bury his bag of gold in the ground. In this context, the term "buried in the ground" means hiding from responsibilities, opportunities, goals and dreams. How do we bury our gold in the ground? It starts with our failure to acknowledge that there are 24 hours in a day.

If we don't acknowledge time, then we won't account for time. The lack of accountability warps our perception of time, and we respond by viewing time as an unlimited resource. Once we view time as an unlimited resource, we are susceptible to excuses that prevent us from meeting our responsibilities, opportunities, goals and dreams. We respond in the same manner as Lazy Steward by hiding our gifts in the ground and returning them to the Creator.

What prompts us to respond this way? It's usually one of these excuses:

1. Failure to Prioritize
2. Distractions
3. Expectations

Failure to Prioritize

When I was in high school, I had an important project due. Instead of finishing the project, I decided to play basketball with my buddies. Knowing that the teacher liked me, I decided to ask for more time to complete the project. To my surprise, my teacher denied my request. I was devastated because my grade suffered from her decision. In anger, I blamed her for my suffering. I remember saying to myself, "couldn't she have given me an extension? I thought she liked me." I didn't realize at the time that my grade suffered, not from my teacher's decision, but from my own decision. I failed to prioritize.

If my project had been important to me, I should have completed it first. In that context, I thought time was an unlimited resource that could be borrowed when needed. I wanted more time to cover my irresponsibility. Time has a beginning and ending, therefore time is limited. My mistake was my failure to prioritize, which led me to push aside what was truly important. Prioritize means to list or rate in order of importance.

Chapter 2 Your Time is Valuable

The importance of a task or opportunity is not determined at the moment of choice. It is determined in the beginning, with a vision of the end in mind. Therefore, prioritizing is the decision to use time on the task or opportunity that we set in the beginning. Failure to prioritize keeps us in a state of confusion. Our desires at the moment are more important than our purpose, and become distractions.

Distractions

The world is filled with many enjoyable and worthwhile pursuits such as education, art, charity, sports, music, entertainment, work, games, etc. At face value, these pursuits are harmless, but when they are placed ahead of our purpose, they become distractions and pull us away from our purpose.

Failure to control distractions is a clear indication that we are no longer focused on reaching an established purpose. When setting goals, it is important to *begin with your focus on the end.* If you follow this principle, you will be able to envision where you want to be and you will take actions that lead you in the direction of your goals. A single-minded focus leads to success.

The world system has learned that your attention is valuable. With that said, the world we live in competes for our attention through a range of distractions -- from sports, telephones, to television, movies, music the list is endless. These pursuits/interests are not bad in and of themselves, but if the time we take to engage in these endeavors takes us away from our higher purpose, they are a distraction to our success. The most popular movies, social media companies, television shows, music, and sports teams earn millions because they garner so much attention from the general population.

As we lose the battle to distractions, we find that we do not have enough time for the things we say we want to accomplish. The world deceives us into welcoming distractions at the expense of purpose. In essence, we turn our actions away from our purpose.

Some of us have learned the importance of purpose, but are unwilling or unable to let go of distractions. In an effort to shift our time between purpose and distraction, we learn to multi-task. Contrary to popular belief, multi-tasking is not the ability to do more than one thing effectively and efficiently at once. Multi-tasking is dividing your attention, time and energy between two or more (usually varied) tasks. We cannot serve two masters. We will love one and hate the other. Purpose requires that you prioritize your time, and focus 100% of your attention. In others words, you will not reach your purpose by alternating time, attention, and energy between purpose and distraction.

Purpose requires focus. When your attention is divided, you will get divided results. For example, let's say that you are preparing for a presentation, but you're also watching television, listening to music, surfing the internet, or chatting on a social website in essence dividing 100% of your energy, time, and attention between tasks.

Multi-tasking vs. Single Tasking

Focus on Preparation- 25%	**100%**
Television- 25%	**Focus on Preparation**
Music – 25%	
Surfing Internet – 25%	

In the table above, if I devote four times (4 * 25%) the energy, time, and attention to preparation, I will have 100% focus.

Let's be clear, I understand that some people use the music as background noise while they work. They actively work on one thing and passively listen to another thing. This helps them concentrate. When I refer to multi-tasking, I mean when you switch between tasks. For instance, you edit a book and surf the internet at the same time, or when you study for 15 minutes, then watch TV for 30 minutes before completing the study period. Your efforts are divided and your results will be less than what they could be.

When you multi-task you condition yourself to accept distraction and not completion as a way of life. You become distracted when you check your email (at dinner or at a social meeting), update your Facebook page (at work), and text (while driving). When you are easily distracted by others, who demand instant responses, you learn how to place the expectations of others above your purpose.

Expectations

Opportunities are all around us. The Stewardship Model helped me see that most people view opportunities differently. Those who are successful are purpose driven view opportunities as vehicles that will help them reach their purpose. That doesn't mean that all of their plans work out the first time. They realize that, moving toward opportunities can maximize results.

On the other hand, those who are unsuccessful fail to take advantage of opportunities because they view opportunities as expectations. This can lead to increased stress and pressure to do something outside of your ability. It creates a burden where relief is found by being inactive and unsuccessful.

Expectations of Others: During my high school years, I was an avid basketball player. My skill didn't reach the level of my passion, but I was fortunate enough to be the starting point guard on my varsity high school team. Basketball at my high school had always trailed football in popularity and attendance. Our school's basketball teams in its entire history had never won more than one-third of its games, but over the summer of my senior year, we made a commitment to change that. When the new season started, we won our first six games in a row, it was the best start in school history. As word spread about our victories, attendance increased and people began to support us. There was even talk about the possibility that our team might be good enough to beat the local basketball powerhouse -- a feat never achieved by our school. The expectations were great and growing each day, but the pressure I placed on myself to win was not healthy.

I remember the game like it was yesterday, with the lead changing back and forth the entire time. With about 20 seconds remaining, our team was losing by one point, with the other team in possession of the ball (in the hands of their all-city point guard who was at least 4 inches taller than I was) there seemed little hope when amazingly I stole the ball from him and started a fast break with the clock winding down. I raced down the middle of the court. Each of our best scorers was closely guarded. It left me a wide-open path to the basket. I didn't know what to do. I was not a scorer, but a great passer with no one to pass the ball to. As the clock started to tick to zero, instead of calling time out, I remembered how the people packed into our gym expecting us to win. So, I took the shot. I missed, and we lost. It was one of the greatest disappointments of my young life and it hounded me for years. In fact, I didn't go to school the next day because I was embarrassed.

What does this have to do with stewardship? I let the expectations of others cloud my judgment, and I took on pressures that were not mine to carry.

Chapter 2 Your Time is Valuable

My purpose was to be the best basketball player that my ability would allow me to be. Winning a game that we've never won against a rival was an expectation of others and too much for my psyche to carry.

When you focus on the expectations of others, fears of failure add a level of performance anxiety not required by the opportunity or the responsibility. Each steward received a bag of gold according to his ability. This leads me to believe that when you operate within your ability and potential to achieve, you can be successful. Anxiety can lead to rushed performances and short cuts. Missed opportunity becomes the norm, and replaces the excellence needed to reach your goals. The steward who received one bag of gold, said, *"I knew that you are a hard man, harvesting where you have not sown and gathering where you have not scattered seed. So I was afraid, went out, and hid your gold in the ground. See, here is what belongs to you."* Sadly, the steward with the one bag created that expectation in his mind. His perception of the Master and his expectations moved him to act in fear and outside of his ability. No one can or wants to perform under a cloud of anxiety.

Expectations of Self: After graduating from college, I landed a job as a Chief Financial Officer. After several years with that company, I decided to become an entrepreneur. Even though I possessed a solid background in financial management, I was not a Certified Public Accountant (CPA). By comparing myself to a CPA, I created expectations for myself that convinced me that I should not pursue my dream. I forgot that my gifts had helped people around me purchase cars and homes. My knowledge helped motivate people to save, invest, and improve their credit. I forgot my unique abilities because I thought I should operate like a CPA firm.

When I forgot my uniqueness, I feared that I wouldn't meet my expectations. Once that happened, it was easy to find excuses not to take advantage of opportunities.

I remained the same and allowed my expectations of self to blind me to who I was and what I could do. This led to a misguided view of time.

The Creator hides treasures in every person. If you allow it, the world system will evaluate you based on what others have done, or what it thinks you should do. At the same time, it will force you to place those expectations on yourself. Basketball star LeBron James, experienced this pressure until he won his first championship in 2012. People wanted to compare him to historical players such as Michael Jordan and Magic Johnson, before he even won his first championship, while others said he would never win one. This was an enormous amount of pressure he faced. Finally, after nine years of frustration, he decided to do two things:

1. **Not compare himself with others**
2. **Insulate himself from the expectations of others**.

Instead of comparing himself to basketball legends and trying to meet the expectation of others, he decided to focus on developing his abilities in order to tap into his own greatness.

When you compare yourself to others and their greatness, you miss all the untapped greatness inside of you. Successful people devote all their heart, mind and strength to pursue their mission and not to what others have done. Successful people consistently manage their time. They understand that time management is essential to complete their daily, weekly and monthly tasks.

Where Does the Time Go?

At least once in our lives, we have all said this common phrase: "I don't have enough time, I need more time". The Lazy Steward ran out of time when the Master returned and settled his accounts with him. The Lazy Steward consumed his time burying his bag of gold in a hole. He did not increase his gold.

Chapter 2 Your Time is Valuable

When you say, "I don't have enough time, I need more time" this is an indication that you value your activities or the activities of others above your advancement. In other words, you want time to fit into your activities and not act as a container for your activities. As I shared earlier, we all operate with 24 hours in a day. Trying to fit 24 hours of time into 25 or more hours of activities can lead to unwise decisions all in an attempt to "get more time." Consumerism, in this context, is an insatiable desire; a belief that you never have enough and always need more. Consumerism generally refers to money, but it can also apply to time. This type of consumerism, adds anxiety, worry and stress to your life. If changes are not made consumerism can have a negative impact on your health in order to pay for your activities.

Enjoy Now and Pay Later

In today's society, if you want to make a purchase, but you cannot afford the item, you don't have to wait until you have the money. There is a way to get what you want now, and pay for it later. It's called borrowing. In this context, borrowing means to continue consumption when you do not have enough resources. Thousands of people take from their future income and are in debt, because they embrace the philosophy of borrowing. There is a relationship between time and money.

The philosophy of consumerism has deceived many into believing that time like money can be borrowed. How many of you have said, "I will do the easy now; and the difficult later". Delaying unpleasant or difficult tasks is procrastination. Procrastination also means consuming time to make life more convenient at the expense of purpose and advancement. Procrastination is the silent killer of dreams.

Procrastination holds back action, yet the clock continues ticking. Each second of delay today, brings greater stress on you tomorrow. This stress can cause you to make poor judgments in an attempt to recapture time lost to procrastination.

Life is hectic enough and just about everyone has felt the crush of time when it comes to schedules and daily tasks, but time need not be a challenge if you can "be faithful."

- Be faithful with your minutes, and you will rule your hours.
- Be faithful with your hours, and you will rule your days.
- Be faithful with your days, and you will rule your weeks.
- Be faithful with your weeks, and you will rule your months.
- Be faithful with your months, and you will rule your years.
- Be faithful with your years, and your life will have meaning and in the end, bear much fruit.

The way we use our time, can lead us toward our purpose or away from it. In the Parable of the Bags of Gold, the Master went away for a long time. He had a schedule, and his servants had to work with his schedule. The Master left enough time for the servants to bring about certain results. Once you understand stewardship, you will realize that you operate on a schedule that is not your own. There is a time to be born and a time to die, but the purpose that we are capable of doing, we can accomplish during our lifetime, that is, if we balance our lives using the correct principles.

BALANCING YOUR LIFE: THE PRINCIPLES

- Diligence
- Punctuality
- Commitment

Diligence

Diligence is work done with careful, steady, energetic effort toward a desired end. In modern times, people view this as hard work, but it's more than the intensity of labor. High intensity labor doesn't guarantee finding a good job, a promotion or suc-

Chapter 2 Your Time is Valuable

cess. Diligence does guarantee that growth because it involves concentration and discipline to focus your mind and efforts towards the desired outcome. Diligence opens the doors of opportunity to success even when people around you overlook your efforts.

Great men and great women make time to think, desire, and plan before they work. With the desired end pictured in their minds they set out to work. Because a diligent man's work and thoughts are towards a desired end, his diligence attracts people to him, and prepares him to stand before people of power and influence. Diligent people operate under the law of sowing and reaping. They see the season and plow with diligence, so that during harvest time, they will have abundance.

In the last chapter, we talked about the law of sowing and reaping. Sowing is planting, and reaping is harvesting or gathering. Simply put, whatever you put in, you get out. Life also works that way. There is no way to bypass this law. Although our society has conditioned us to accept "microwaving" as a standard (meaning we invest little time or energy in life) for great results. For example, if we gorge ourselves with food, over time we will gain weight.

In an effort to lose the weight quickly, we try questionable weight loss measures such as pills or fad diets all in an attempt to take time out of the equation. Bypassing the process is not how life is designed to work, and can have negative consequences.

One reason the Lazy Steward was afraid was because he was unwilling to commit to the process. The process is ownership and growth. He believed that he could be successful remaining the same. To reach a level of success, in accordance with his ability, the Lazy Steward needed to exercise careful, steady, and energetic effort towards an expected end. Burying a bag of gold in a hole required very little work and even less concentration and discipline. From the start, his attention was not on growth.

The Growing of You

In life, diligence during the process is required to reach the desired outcome. New Year's Day resolutions are commonly a time where people make a declaration to permanently change their behavior. But, declaring that you will change is only part of the equation. It takes twenty-one days of repeated behavior to establish a habit. When a seed is planted and a season of (diligent plowing) growth occurs, it is followed by a harvest or gathering at the appointed time. Life is not happenstance; it is governed by the seasons, as in planting and harvesting. Those who prosper understand this principle. They prepare themselves during the process for the harvest of success at the appointed time.

Punctual Scheduling

Our lives are filled with a myriad of tasks (e.g. cooking, working, entertainment, volunteering, and child care) that command our attention. Because we have many different responsibilities and distractions that we consider enjoyable or urgent, we sometimes put off what we can do today --until tomorrow. Sometimes it's the very thing that we put off that is the means for our success.

How many of us, in need of losing weight, like to say that we will start our diet, or exercise regimen on Monday, and when Monday comes, we have an excuse for not following through? Delay is not limited to losing weight. Starting a new project, or studying for a test always appear to work out better tomorrow than today. Isn't it ironic that when resolutions are made they are scheduled to begin on New Year's Day and not immediately?

The understanding of the relationship between time and important tasks is necessary to be successful. Generally, our time is commanded by those things in life that are enjoyable or urgent. We must learn that there are times when we need to drop what we are doing to work on the important task and not the enjoyable or urgent tasks. Let's face it, some people simply do not do a good job of scheduling their time, and as a result, they

Chapter 2 Your Time is Valuable

end up focusing on urgent tasks and they forsake important tasks. Enjoyable and urgent tasks distract you from important tasks that pull you to a higher place; a place of rulership, a place where you are a conqueror. An urgent life brings about stress, anxiety, and fear, while an important life is one of fulfillment and purpose.

With the creation of a schedule, you assign priority to an important task. In the parable of the bags of gold, whatever tasks the Good Stewards were focused on, prior to receiving their gold, became secondary. The important task of managing and increasing the bags of gold became their main purpose or goal. Good Stewards assigned priority to their tasks and realized the benefit of time and important tasks working together. The Lazy Steward did not make the important task primary and as a result, buried his bag of gold in a hole within the time given; therefore, he had a lot of time to be afraid and no time to accomplish his task. He failed to be punctual.

Punctuality is the characteristic of moving at once within the available timeframe. This is a key to being successful with purpose.

When faced with an important task, start it, even if you are unable to finish it in the allotted timeframe. Moving at once is the connection to faith. The longer you delay, the idea and inspiration to work begins to fade from your mind and your heart. Have you ever had a new idea and instead of writing it down, you decided that you didn't need to, because you would remember such a grand idea? What happened?

By failing to move at once and write down the idea within the timeframe given there's a good chance that you forgot it. I learned this lesson the hard way and now I always keep a means for recording my thoughts and ideas at a moment's notice. The Lazy Steward lost his bag of gold to the Good Steward with ten bags of gold because he failed to move within the available timeframe. It's the same with our life's purpose. Each of us is given a set time to fulfill our life's purpose. We don't know how much time we have to fulfill our life's purpose, but we have more than enough time to do so, if we move at once.

An interesting observation of the parable was that there was no interaction between the Good Stewards and the Lazy Steward during the time the Master was gone on his long journey. Even though they were all together when the Master called them, after receiving the bags of gold, the Good Stewards went at once, while the Lazy Steward went off. When you are punctual with purpose, punctuality will separate you from those who are not.

Commitment

Several years ago, prior to writing the "Growing of You," I decided that my objective would be to become a professional motivational speaker. I developed a schedule and believed that I was prepared to embark on this exciting new career. Well, life didn't assist me in the manner I had hoped. My financial management business experienced a decline, significantly reducing my income.

My attention went from becoming a professional motivational speaker, to trying to determine how I could replace the lost income. Replacing that income proved more difficult than I thought, and soon I was no longer following the schedule that I developed. What happened? Why didn't I continue following the schedule while making other efforts to meet my immediate need for income? I had forgotten my commitment to purpose. The definition of commitment is an agreement or promise to do something.

I developed the time schedule for reaching my goal of becoming a professional motivational speaker, but I neglected to adhere to my commitment on a daily basis. Some days, I would practice for an hour. On "good days" when the state of my income did not make me anxious, or when I felt inspired, I would practice for two hours.

Chapter 2 Your Time is Valuable

On "lazy days" when an outside force disturbed me, I stopped working for days, sometimes weeks. I gave the environment control over my progress. This example describes "interested people" who will work until a change in their environment derails their progress. Each day you should work on developing your gift not just when it is convenient for you. What I mean is trials, obstacles, and environment will come to test your resolve. Without that understanding, it's easy to interpret changes in the environment as evidence that you cannot progress—and that is far from the truth. My schedule should have been in control, not my environment. If my schedule required two hours of practice for five days a week, then *nothing* should interrupt that time.

Scheduling is the plan and commitment is the power behind your effort

To overcome the obstacles, hindrances or trials will require commitment. Having commitment goes beyond simple interest in the success of the plan. The success of the plan requires sacrifice.

Sacrifice is a transition from interest to commitment. Will you stop at your interest or proceed with commitment?

- Interested people (IP) don't invest money; Committed people (CP) do
- IP participate only if time permits; CP make time to participate
- IP succumb to temporary distraction; CP embrace a permanent mission

When you set out to do a task, do you start with zeal and passion, only later to be derailed by circumstances? Life happens to everyone. I learned firsthand that life doesn't always work within the framework of our plans, nor does it always allow us to catch up. My choices were to live life limited by loss, or live life influenced by potential.

In order to stay on schedule I needed a DEEP commitment.

Desire - The power of attraction. It motivates you to move toward your destination and pulls your destination to you.

Endurance - The power to not give in to hardship, adversity and pain en route to your destination.

Excellence - The power to give your best with all your heart.

Persistence - The power to continue in a course of action in spite of opposition.

When you make a DEEP commitment, you become empowered to reach your goal. No longer will circumstances affect your decisions.

Your decisions will create circumstances that are in line with what you desire. You are a created being filled with creative power. As created beings, we operate in a world where the general mindset is that things will always be as they have always been. Things *will* always be as they have always been if we allow them. The creative power within us enables us to create.

Commitment is the effort to create. We must remember that creation is the investment of time and effort. Time serves a dual purpose. On one hand, time management enables us to accomplish daily tasks. On the other hand, time investment allows us to develop ourselves.

Time stewardship requires a *commitment to use time effectively* and a *schedule* to use time efficiently.

Chapter 2 Your Time is Valuable

Effectiveness (purpose)

The Effective Steward uses time as a tool to create. In order to create, the Effective Steward's viewpoint is future-oriented. He is purpose driven, viewing tomorrow through the eyes of today. To that end, the Effective Steward sets aside time to seed his mind, to create his desired reality. You reap what you sow; whatever thoughts you allow to settle in your mind, creates that reality for you.

The world we live in is not a true sense of reality, but a reflection of the reality we create or have allowed to be created. This misunderstanding can have a great impact on how we use our time. Have you ever faced a situation that seemed insurmountable, you said to yourself, "Why waste time trying to change the situation"? Developing a true sense of reality requires time to create it first in your mind. For the purpose of effective time stewardship, we must begin by devoting time to the seven building blocks of creation used by Effective Stewards called the "Power of One".

Each of us possesses these building blocks, but in order to successfully utilize them, time must be devoted to each one until we learn to use the seven in unison:

- Imagination
- Visualization
- Goals
- Thoughts
- Emotion
- Desire
- Action

We will cover the "Power of One" in more detail in chapter four. At this point, you should understand that the future is created in your mind first and by your hand later. The Effective Steward is willing to put in the time to create the proper internal belief system. This is important, because sometimes the path to growth starts from less than desirable circumstances. You may be broken, discouraged, disillusioned, or even imprisoned. It really doesn't matter where you are physically as long as you can daily devote time to the "Power of One". It serves as the foundation for change and the inspiration for growth. I'm sure that you have heard the stories of people who were in hopeless situations, but over time they were inspired to change and grow. People who lost weight, went back to school, started a business, or bought a house whether or not they understood their motivation, the path they followed was directed by the "Power of One".

To say it succinctly, believe in yourself and set aside time to practice. Be passionate about learning, getting better, and advancing. Thomas Aquinas, a 13th century priest and philosopher said, "Repetition is the mother of learning". The more you perform a task, you increase the probability that your proficiency will increase. Rehearse and repeat is the mantra of the Effective Steward.

The greatest challenge you face as an Effective Steward is that you have to walk by faith, and not by sight. In other words, you must pursue growth without physical evidence that such growth is possible. That is why the building blocks of creation are so valuable. I can't stress the importance of holding a picture of what you desire in your mind. If you can't see it in your mind, you will never create it in your life. By exercising the "Power of One" daily you greet each day with a mental picture of what you desire to accomplish.

Efficiency (Balance)

The Efficient Steward's viewpoint of time is focused on the maintenance of his life. For him, life is a balance between time, resources, and action. He realizes time; resources and action are valuable and should be handled accordingly. In response he seeks to operate within those limits to make life as predictable and manageable as possible. In order to operate in this manner, the Efficient Steward creates lists with tasks for completion and schedules to allocate time for completion. The use of lists and schedules guide his actions, based on the fact that his time and resources are limited. Because he recognizes the value of these things, he "Counts up the Cost" of how he uses his time, resources, and action.

In "Counting up the Cost" the Efficient Steward evaluates the cost of his time and resources before engaging in action. The objective is to receive the maximum benefit while using a predictable and manageable process. This process is known as "Counting up the Cost" and is based on three questions:

1. What needs to be done?
2. What resources are available?
3. What are the minimal resources needed to complete the job correctly?

The Efficient Steward answers these questions prior to taking action. He plans today how he will manage his time, resources and actions tomorrow. As much as possible, surprises will not catch him unprepared, because he knows that they cost time and resources. So, the Efficient Steward plans for the appropriate action, and leaves time and resources available for situations and circumstances that he was unable to predict, and therefore makes them manageable.

Conflicted Viewpoints

The Effective Steward creates what he needs, while the Efficient Steward manages what he has. We were born with the ability to operate in both views, but the pains we face in life normally cause us to gravitate to the one viewpoint that is most comfortable and sacrifice the one which is uncomfortable. The over reliance on one viewpoint creates weakness in us that develops from the absence of the other.

If you are an Effective Steward, you are focused on building a future through growth. Your perception is that the pursuit of development allows no time for activities. This drive helps you accomplish great things. However, the Effective Steward's use of time to practice is often at the expense of using time to accomplish other activities that together make for a rewarding life.

Ironically, the things that the Effective Steward spends time on, creates results, but what he avoids spending time on, also creates consequences. The consequences of improper nutrition and inadequate sleep are poor health. The consequences of avoiding people are broken relationships or no relationships. The Effective Steward accomplishes great results, but at a cost. For what shall it profit a man to gain the whole world only to lose his soul?

The Efficient Steward's greatest weakness is that he places a greater focus on present activities. Your perception is that you have to get everything done now. In today's society, an increasing number of people are trying to do and focus on more activities. Social networking, news feeds, cell phones, texting, email, and other gadgetry cause the Efficient Steward to be connected, leading to an overload of information. The focus is no longer on one thing at one time, but on everything all the time.

When people try to do more and focus on everything, this draws their attention to multiple sources resulting in an increase in multi-tasking as a solution. The Efficient Steward will never complete all his activities, because of how he perceives time. With the focus on the limitations of life, an Efficient Steward can quickly learn to over-emphasize the importance of the task and under-emphasize the importance of growth.

Purpose and Balance

Are you an effective person who seeks success through focus on future growth, or an efficient person who seeks success through focus on managing resources today? Success is based on effectiveness and efficiency. The path to success calls for focusing time to take care of the present responsibilities, <u>and</u> creating the future you desire by living a balanced life.

Chapter 2 Your Time is Valuable

How do you make yourself a success? Learn to greet each day with a plan, but no ordinary plan, a two-fold plan that I call "Purpose and Balance". Solomon, the wise king once wrote:

"There is a time for everything, and a season for every activity under heaven:

- a time to be born and a time to die,
- a time to plant and a time to uproot,
- a time to kill and a time to heal,
- a time to tear down and a time to laugh,
- a time to mourn and a time to dance,
- a time to scatter stones and a time to gather them,
- a time to embrace and a time to refrain,
- a time to search and a time to give up,
- a time to keep and a time to throw away,
- a time to tear and a time to mend,
- a time to be silent and a time to speak,
- a time to love and a time to hate,
- a time for war and a time for peace.

What would life be like if there was only a time to be born or a time to die? Without a time to be born, there would be no life on Earth, and without a time to die, there would not be enough resources for everyone who has ever lived.

Which choice would you make between a time to be silent and a time to speak? Imagine if everyone was silent all the time, or worse, if everyone talked all the time. In like manner, there is a time for purpose and a time for balance.

The Good Steward uses "Purpose and Balance" to effectively create, and then efficiently manage the time and resources for that day. This process creates a cycle of abundance that includes management and increase. My personal "Purpose and Balance" plan calls for me to start each day at least two hours before I normally need to wake up. This time allows me to follow the steps of the "Power of One" to create the future I desire.

Next, I follow my plan to complete those activities needed for that day. Then, at the end of the work day, I allocate time for personal recreation/rest. Finally, before I go to bed, I set a plan for the next day's activities starting with the "Power of One".

Good Stewards understand the dual nature of Purpose and Balance. Stewards who manage their time well are some of the busiest people, yet they also get the most tasks done while achieving great success. They have learned to make the most of their time by learning to say no to those tasks and requests that are simply not important to them, and yes to those things that matter. The ability to say no, keeps them from being overly involved in tasks, requests and mundane activities. This discipline allows them to say yes to practice, study, and growth.

The Effective Steward views time as a creator pursuing purpose; while the Efficient Steward views time as a way to maintain balance. In order to be a successful Good Steward, we must view Purpose and Balance as a whole, to be fruitful and multiply.

Be Fruitful

After each steward received his bag of gold, the Good Stewards went at once and put their money to work. They wanted to prosper and produced good results. Today, our lives are no different, in that we desire to prosper, but unfortunately, like the Lazy Steward, the mindset of some people is not on production or being fruitful. Using the 80/20 rule as a basis, 20% of stewards use time to be **<u>productive</u>** and 80% spend their time existing. I say existing, instead of living because living (life) is about change, it is about growth. In the end, they succumb to life's distractions: the big game, the new movie, the big sale or so many other things that pre-empt their time to practice, study and advance.

Life is not all about convenience and enjoyment alone. Life includes accomplishments. We must not take time for granted. If you talk to people who are older and more experienced, at

Chapter 2 Your Time is Valuable

some point in the conversation they would likely tell you that if they could go back in time, they would not have waited to pursue their goals and dreams.

In their youth, they wanted convenience and enjoyment. They believed they would have enough time to "enjoy now" and "produce later." Those same people are now discouraged because they fear they won't have enough time to accomplish their dreams. The good news is that you can still maximize the time you have left and not worry about what has past. Carry forward the lesson from the past and do not allow the pain of it to be applied in the present. Commit to being productive in worthwhile endeavors.

What are some worthwhile endeavors in your life?

What do you want to accomplish?
Earn a college degree, start a business, get a better job, or become a better financial steward.

Who do you want to help?
Volunteer for charitable causes, extend financial and professional support to organizations, or mentor children.

What changes do you want to see in your life?
Lose weight, exercise, stop smoking, or eat healthy.

Engaging in worthwhile endeavors allows the world to see how fruitful you are. Within you lies the ability to take a worthwhile endeavor and multiply the results.

The Principle of Multiplication

The man who had received the five bags of gold brought the other five. *"Master," he said, "you entrusted me with five bags of gold. See, I have gained five more."* Matthew 25:20

"The man with two bags of gold also came. 'Master,' he said, 'you entrusted me with two bags of gold; see, I have gained two more.' Matthew 25:22

Each steward received at least one bag of gold, according to his ability to procure an increase. The stewards, who received five and two bags of gold, respectively decided that they would devote their time to putting their money to work. The other steward decided to consume time by hiding his talent until his Master returned. This approach is symbolic of people who spend time, and maybe their entire lives, trying to avoid doing the Master's work. After a time, the Master returned and settled the accounts with them. Much to his delight, two of the stewards had doubled his money. The other steward returned his bag of gold to the Master unchanged.

What separates the Good Stewards from the Lazy Stewards? The Good Stewards "went at once and put their money to work and gained more" while the Lazy Steward "went away, dug a hole and hid his money. The Good Stewards understood that they were multipliers. A multiplier is one who understands that he has the power to multiply. In order to multiply, you must exercise proper thoughts, actions and use of time to position yourself to multiply. These are tools that build and serve as the foundation of any great work. A multiplier who possesses a college degree takes his thoughts, actions and time to multiply the value of that degree. He will not expect the accomplishment of the degree to be the end, but the beginning.

The more time you invest in a worthwhile endeavor, the greater the results. This means that you achieve long lasting results in a shorter period. Practice (the investment of thought, action, and time) makes perfect; and the investment (of money) makes you wealthy. If you invest time learning how money works, and apply the correct action of investing, then your money multiplies based on the understanding, potential, and resources you started with and the amount of time you applied what you learned.

The application of time toward a worthwhile endeavor is the key ingredient for advancement and increase.

Chapter 2 Your Time is Valuable

During the time that passed, the Good Stewards applied purposeful thought and action to a worthwhile endeavor. Anyone can operate this principle, but only Good Stewards will use their time to advance and increase.

Summary

There are 24 hours in a day. Proper investment of time can take what is ordinary or average and by multiplication, transform it into something extraordinary and great, resulting in expertise or rulership.

Consumerism is a belief that you never have enough and you always need more. Trying to fit time into your activities leads you to make unwise decisions in an effort to "get more time."

Procrastination means to consume time, in order to make life more convenient at the expense of purpose. Life is not all convenience and enjoyment, a major part of life is accomplishment. Procrastination is the silent killer of dreams. It holds back action, yet the clock continues ticking. Each second of delay brings greater stress on you. Expectations add a level of pressure to perform that opportunity does not require. The results are often rushed performances or short cuts to success.

The misuse of time manifests through failure to prioritize, distractions, and an excessive focus on expectations. The failure to prioritize leads to the avoidance of what is important. Distractions pull away from purpose, and your focus is no longer on the desired outcome.

Time stewardship involves the use of time consistent with your established mission in life, requiring both a *schedule* of your time for management and a *commitment* (pledge) of your time to practice for increase and discovery of your purpose. A *commitment* is an agreement, or promise to do something in the future. When you make a DEEP commitment to yourself, you are able to empower your efforts.

- **D**esire is the power of attraction.
- **E**ndurance is the power to proceed through hardship.
- **E**xcellence is the power to give your best with all your heart.
- **P**ersistence is the power to continue in the face of opposition.

Chapter 3
Your Ability is Valuable

Acknowledge – the power of your gift
Accept responsibility - to fulfill your purpose
Affirm – to develop your potential
Act – to describe and connect with the world.

Believe in Yourself Again

As a child, I loved numbers. I could add, subtract, multiply and divide in my head from a young age. As I got older, my love of numbers manifested itself in a unique way. I could remember numbers without paying attention. I could shop in the grocery stores, and without writing down prices, be able to compare with what I saw on the shelf. There were many times when I alerted the manager to an incorrectly priced item, and as a result, I received the item free under the store's price guarantee policy. This gift served me well during the financial lean times but I failed to use the gift in line with my ability. For years I avoided any opportunity to work professionally in the financial arena. My ability was hidden until a former mentor encouraged me to use my gifts and talents in line with my ability. Looking back, I can see how a simple love of numbers is in fact a gift that continues to benefit me and others. This is personal stewardship.

Stewardship is the faithful, prudent and profitable use of one's gifts and talents in line with their ability. Each of us has talents and gifts so that we can make the world a better place. In addition, Personal Stewardship encourages us to interact with others as we learn to transition from doubting our gifts, to accepting them and using them. The responsible use of our gifts and talents allows us to connect with others and change the world.

The opposition to Personal Stewardship is the deceptive belief that your gift cannot benefit others. What words are you hearing, or have heard that stop you from utilizing your personal gifts? The voice of opposition often belongs to other people. This voice can create mindsets, influence perceptions and reinforce belief systems that cause the words of others, your lack of experience, or your negative personal experience with people you trusted define you and leave you fearful of using your gift in line with your ability.

My advice is to gain experience in settings that will allow you to develop confidence in the areas where you possess gifts. I love basketball and during my teenage years, there were times when I played with people who were more skilled than I and as result, I became discouraged when I compared my talent level to theirs. There was one player in particular who I viewed as being college-level talent. Whenever I played against him in high school, he outplayed me. After I graduated, I decided that I would develop my basketball skills. I began to practice with people who were similar in talent level. After a few months, I found myself on the basketball court facing my high school rival. During the game I discovered something, he could no longer outplay me. In fact, I outplayed him. I had grown beyond my opposition.

This growth came from confidence developed from using my talent with others of similar talent level. It was then that I felt comfortable facing more growth challenges from those I thought were slightly above me.

The growth challenge faced by the Lazy Steward was not from external sources, but from the obstacles he created in his mind; while the Good Stewards used their gifts in line with their abilities and each faithfully gained five and two bags of gold. The Lazy Steward's perception of his ability and experiences with the Master was in opposition to who he could be. His perceptions lead him to hide his abilities and gifts from the world. Examine your perceptions about yourself or a situation.

Chapter 3 Your Ability is Valuable

If you change your perceptions, you will change your results. Are you settling for a boring, predictable and mundane life when you can astound yourself by the things you desire and are capable of doing? There are three types of opposition that shape your perceptions and influence your behavior incorrectly, internal opposition, circumstantial opposition and people centered opposition.

Internal Opposition: Your internal world is a barrier to you seeing who you really are:

Envy: There is a fine line between a healthy respect and admiration of someone else's gift and envying someone else's gift. You can overcome envy by seeing the value in what you have. Believe me, there is someone who can benefit from what you have to offer. Search out people in your social circle to see who can benefit from your gift. Envy is no longer an opposition when you learn to value:

- what you have
- what you can do

Unforgiveness: Failure is not a measure of your gift. It is the reality of your humanity. Everyone has tried something and failed, but not everyone responds to failure in the same way. Some people view failure as a tool for evaluation, while others use failure as a weapon to punish themselves for their error. This kind of self-torment can lead to depression and the unwillingness to try again. Forgive yourself. Your humanity will never reach perfection, and you should not hold the value of your gift against unattainable standards.

Note: I did not say standards of excellence, which is the power to give your best with all of your heart.

Circumstantial Opposition: Circumstances that keep you from seeing who you are:

Lack of Money: Money is not an evaluator of the successful use of a gift, growth is. Growth will bring about money. Even Kobe Bryant once played basketball for free, but the absence of money, did not stop him from growing. He believed in his ability and continued to practice his gift which brought him earnings in the hundreds of millions of dollars.

Can you see who you are and not what you lack? Once you see who you are, you will not lack. If you spend time obsessing over money or the lack of it, you oppose your gifts and hinder their development. Life is about creation, growth, and change. Existence means to continue to be. It takes food, water, clothing, and shelter to exist and these things come by possessing money. But if you are not careful, the lack of money can cause you to shift your focus from seeing who you are to simply trying to exist. I'm not saying that existence is not important it's simply that it should not be at the forefront of your purpose.

Focusing solely on existing, is the classic "cart before the horse syndrome". You exist for a purpose. Keep your eyes on your purpose and life will bring the resources you need to exist. With only $100 in my pocket, I moved to Sarasota with my eyes on purpose and shortly after my arrival a new job and housing became available. Trust that you exist for a purpose and purpose will lead to opportunities to maintain your existence.

Lack of Opportunity: I have learned that gifts can make room for you. By this I mean that, there is an "internal mechanism" that attracts and connects your gifts to opportunity. Don't focus on the perceived lack of opportunity. Problems arise when you focus on the perceived lack of opportunity during the time you should be using your gifts in line with your ability that will attract opportunity.

People Centered Opposition: People oppose your progress:

Comparisons to Others: Who do *you* say men are? When you compare yourself to others, it blinds you to the money, talent, time, and opportunity that you already possess.

Chapter 3 Your Ability is Valuable

Stewardship gives you insight to embrace who you *are* instead of comparing yourself to who you are not. Comparison is not wise and can surely create opposition that hinders you from reaching your greatness. Think about it, when you say that you are not as good as someone else, your comparison creates a barrier of opposition to your greatness blocking what you have to offer the world.

Word Programming: Who do men say you are? When someone says something about you that is *not true*, do you believe them? Have you let hurdles and barriers prevent you from moving up or moving forward? There will be gainsayers (people who speak ill about you) in spite of the good you do. They talk about you in an attempt to make you ineffective. Their goal is to subject *you* to the power of their words and not to the power, potential and purpose within you. These gainsayers do not have the authority or expertise to evaluate you in this manner. In certain situations those who do have authority over you (parents, teachers, or employers) will use authority through the prism of their own failures as a way to convince you that you cannot reach your goals. Be careful of people whose words only tear down and never build up. Their words reveal their nature. It requires no skill to tear down, but requires great skill to build up.

Company You Keep: The people you are around can create opposition to your goals. It's been said that "birds of a feather flock together". This means that you are the company you keep. If not so immediately, you will be so eventually. When the company you keep operates in a manner that is contrary to your goals this creates opposition and loss.

Keep in mind that what you have experienced in life does not define who you are; and likewise, the things you have lost do not define who you are. Each person encounters his or her own form of opposition. In fact, opposition is a sign that you have great potential. The path to purpose often requires you to go through opposition. So many people give up at the first sign of opposition, when in fact this is the first checkpoint to their purpose.

The Growing of You

Will you stop and surrender, or stand and fight the opposition? If you do not have the money, find it. If you do not have opportunity, create one. If you do not have the support of others, support yourself or find others who do.

Each of us has the potential to prosper through our purpose. The gifts and talents within you are evidence of who you really are. The vehicle by which we unleash that potential is stewardship. Make no mistake, opposition is painful. It will make some of you hide your ability, and others to find a more pleasurable substitute. The question remains whether or not you allow the pain of opposition to stop you. To move beyond where opposition has limited you requires that you do something most people are unwilling to do. Acknowledge that your present effort is not stronger than the opposition. In order to overcome, you will have to submit to the *Growing of You*, and accept that your past efforts were not sufficient, change and pursue your desired outcome for as long as it takes, give as much as it takes, and persist even when there is resistance.

Persistence

Thomas Edison's pursuit to create the electric filament was an example of persistence. During an interview he was asked, *"How does it feel having failed over 2,000 times trying to create the electric filament?"* This went well beyond the time he expected results, but he did not let the lack of results stop him. Edison responded by saying, *"I have not failed, not once. I have discovered 10,000 ways that do not work."* What a great attitude toward persistence. He simply kept going, until he succeeded by inventing a device that has changed the modern world.

Persistence is the key that unlocks and opens doors. It helps the gift within you bring change to the world even if the world does not understand its need for your gift. If you want to see a change in the people around you, then you must continue to move forward in spite of indifference from others. Here is a parable that illustrates that point.

Chapter 3 Your Ability is Valuable

"Suppose one of you has a friend, and he goes to him at midnight and says, 'Friend, lend me three loaves of bread, because a friend of mine on a journey has come to me, and I have nothing to set before him.' "Then the one inside answers, 'Don't bother me. The door is already locked, and my children are with me in bed. I can't get up and give you anything.' I tell you, though he will not get up and give him the bread because he is his friend, yet because of the man's boldness (or persistence) he will get up and give him as much as he needs. " Luke 11: 5-8 NIV

In the parable the one who wanted to borrow the three loaves of bread could help his friend on a journey, but his friend in the house was indifferent to the borrower, because to assist him would cause discomfort. The borrower was able to *see beyond resistance*. What he saw beyond resistance was the desired outcome. Persistence means that you believe that the power behind your desired outcome is greater than that which resists you. The irony is, persistence disrupts the status quo. The world will respond to your persistence and open the door to meet your needs, so that you can meet the needs of others.

Patience Endurance

Have you ever wanted something, but the challenge was so great that it was easier to give up? I have. This book is a work of faith and patience, and by patience I mean endurance and mental toughness to grow. Growth is not an easy task, but is a necessary one. We are literally made to grow. Life has entrusted us with time, talent, and financial resources to facilitate that growth.

There were many, many times when I started writing this book and then stopped because of an opposition that overwhelmed my desire to grow. Faith starts your journey, but patient endurance helps you hold on until the end. Picture a famous marathon like the New York City Marathon where thousands of people participate in this 26-mile grueling race. Some runners train and are strong, while others are fast.

The fact that these runners even participated is evidence that they have the faith they can finish. Although thousands of people start the race, not everyone will finish. They won't finish because they lack patient endurance to make it through the middle or toughest part of the race. How can you tell if you lack patient endurance? If you quit when faced with opposition and trials, then your patience is small and you have not allowed it to grow. You may have faith to move mountains, but lack the endurance to exercise that faith to the end in spite of trouble or adversity.

People who lack endurance begin to complain and stop believing. They become bitter, discouraged and they blame the world for their failure because they have been unable to accomplish their goals. It is important that you do not respond with a complaint. It is important that you face adversity with joy knowing that if you endure with patience success will come for you as it did for Edison.

It is important to be mentally tough when faced with adversity. Adversity may cause you to pause, but do not let it stop you from moving up and forward. Hold on because the pain from adversity is the catalyst for growth. Growth is a process. Do not look for an escape; be resolved to persevere through adversity and your mental toughness will grow and nothing can stop you from accomplishing what you desire. The pain from adversity will be forgotten when you reach your goal.

Perseverance

Perseverance is your commitment not to allow anything to convince you to stop short of your purpose. You have been given great power to reach your destination and nothing can stop you from fulfilling your purpose unless you stop because of a distraction. Distraction is a natural enemy to perseverance. It tempts us to stop. The distractions may satisfy you for a season, but persevering to reach the desires of your heart will satisfy you for a lifetime.

Chapter 3 Your Ability is Valuable

The desires of the heart are those things that God put in your heart to accomplish. Your heart attracts what it needs to fulfill your purpose, but if your heart is distracted from your purpose, you will repel what you should attract. Life pads your path with resistance in the form of temptations, distractions, and discouragement in order to convince you to stop short of your purpose. To overcome that resistance requires perseverance. The fuel of perseverance is peace of mind. Without peace of mind, the commitment can wane because you are discouraged by the less than desirable outcome you may be presently experiencing. There is a power stronger than you. That power may be friends with positive attitudes, prayer, inspirational readings, or meditation. Each can provide you with what you need to continue persevering to your purpose.

Perseverance does not *determine* how great you are; perseverance *reveals* how great you are. Champions persevere against resistance. It's what sets LeBron James apart from many of his contemporaries. There are a number of great basketball players in the NBA today, but fewer champions.

LeBron became a champion when he persevered to reveal his greatness. From high school, he was anointed the next great basketball player of his generation, but he learned the hard way that there is a difference between a great player and a champion. He thought he could bypass the growth and rely on talent alone during his tenure with the Cleveland Cavaliers, but soon discovered that talent didn't guarantee a championship. After leaving his team in Cleveland to play for the Miami Heat, his second trip to the finals, like the first, ended in defeat.

He learned that by simply surrounding himself with great players, would not guarantee a championship. His transformation into a champion was complete when he committed to perseverance; committed to becoming the best LeBron James that he could be instead of resting on the laurels bestowed on him by pundits as the greatest basketball player of his generation. The following two years after his loss in the NBA finals, he won two consecutive regular season and NBA finals Most Valuable Player awards in route to becoming a two-time champion. Champions persevere against resistance. The joy of succeeding inspires them to persevere. Champions ignore temptations, distractions and discouragement to complete whatever they set their hearts to do because perseverance is the fuel of faithfulness, and will enable them to reach their destination.

Faithfulness

In our youth, we greet the world with our gifts and a solid belief in them. We keep this faith-filled outlook until we experience failure or ridicule from others. As a result, we retreat into a shell no longer true to ourselves. We stopped being faithful because we stopped doing what was given to us to do. Faithfulness means that you are trusted to get the job done. In practical terms you

1. accept your gifts and their uniqueness
2. believe in the value of your ability
3. take action to work your gifts to the best of your ability

This is your original and unimpaired condition. It's a key component for the "Growing of You". The path to your greatness begins with the confidence to use your gifts. Without the confidence to exercise your gifts, burying them in a hole will appear to be a viable option. From ages 10 to 17, I was a sought-after public speaker. It wasn't until an embarrassing situation in college, in which I forgot my lines that fear set in and I lost my confidence. After that experience, I began to fear what might happen during future speaking engagements. Would I flub my lines, or forget them altogether. My fear became my reality, and once onstage, I sometimes forgot parts of my presentation. After a few of these embarrassing incidents, I stopped all public speaking until I learned to believe in the value of my gift. This lesson helped me understand that my gift's value was not to be proven, but revealed when I treasured it enough to consistently use it. Victory does not happen during competition, it happens during the preparation.

Chapter 3 Your Ability is Valuable

Great people use what they have, are motivated by what they expect to have, in order to pursue what they do not have.

Michael Jordan, one of the greatest professional basketball players of our time, became a six-time champion with this preparation mindset. Like most basketball athletes, Michael Jordan possessed remarkable physical abilities. What separated Jordan from the rest and made him a great champion was his understanding of how much better he could perform with preparation. He believed that faithfulness to practice would make him the greatest player ever, and his belief prompted him to practice. He demonstrated that consistent practice leads to high degrees of success. I remember an article in which Jordan, describing his contemporaries, said he knew that he was better when he saw how lax his competitors were in practice. He knew that pure talent could take them only so far. Practice separates high achievers from those who are mediocre.

In the parable of the bags of gold, each steward received at least one bag of gold from the Master. The Master had faith in each servant's ability and faithfulness to increase the value of the bags of gold. Two of them faithfully performed works with great results. For the parable said, *"The man who had received five bags of gold went at once and put his money to work and gained five bags more. So also, the one with two bags of gold gained two more."* Even when you do not see how your gift will bring about the results you seek, the faithful use can help you reach your potential.

For example, let's say that you have a gift for cooking, and the thing you hope for is to become a chef; the fact that you possess the gift is the evidence of the potential to become a chef. Or, let's say that you have a propensity for fixing things, and the thing you hope for is to become an engineer or mechanic, the fact that you possess the gift is the evidence of the potential for you to become an engineer or mechanic. The gifts are the evidence of potential not seen, and the substance of success hoped for.

Responsibility

Have you ever started a project, but failed to complete it? I am sure most of you will say yes. In fact, I'm sure most of you even have a reason for why you failed to complete the task. But when you fail to complete a task, you are not being responsible. Responsibility is more than accepting accountability, it is responding in accordance to your ability. Let me explain.

Starting a task or mission is easy. How many times have you promised yourself that you would clean the garage, or learn a foreign language? And how many times have you failed to even start?

The more times you promise that you will do something, but you fail to start and complete it, the easier it becomes to accept defeat as a standard outcome. If your gifts are not enough to complete a task, don't stop, continue moving forward building your ability along the way.

My challenge to you is that you no longer walk at the world's pace, but learn how to walk at your own pace. Respond based on your ability. Pace is the rate of activity, progress, growth, performance and tempo. In establishing true stewardship, walking in your own pace is the key to bringing about the responsibility needed to be a Good Steward:

- Possession
- Accountability
- Control
- Exercise

Possession: is to focus on what you have, and not on what you lack. Countless people avoid their purpose because they do not believe they have what it takes to succeed. The truth is, in some arenas, greater talent and more money would make things easier to obtain, but possessions alone are not the determining factors to being a Good Steward. An understanding of what you possess is essential.

Chapter 3 Your Ability is Valuable

Accountability: is to have an obligation to report to one in authority over you. You have been given, talent, and money and you must be faithful with what you have received.

Control: is to exercise restraint or direction over; to dominate; command time, talent and money. You have 24 hours in a day, and you have been given a gift, skill or ability. The problems that hinder the manifestation of your greatness are related to your lack of control in one or more of these areas.

- A lack of control in money. You spend more than you take in, or you do not bring in enough.

- A lack of control in ability. You allow the opinions of others, or their failures to determine how you use your ability.

- A lack of control in time. You engage in frivolous pursuits allowing others to control your time.

Exercise: is action, use, operation, or effect. Your commitment to proper stewardship of your time, talent, and money prompts the action and effort needed to deliver your ability to the world.

Learn from the Lazy Steward who received one bag of gold, but instead of working to increase his holdings, he dug a hole and hid his Master's money.

He failed to complete one action (increasing the Master's money) before starting another (digging a hole to bury the bag). His failure to complete a task not only disqualified him from rulership, but caused him to lose the bag of gold he was given.

Whenever I reveal that I am an author and professional motivational speaker, people express their own fear of public speaking by making statements such as:

The Growing of You

- I'm afraid that I would embarrass myself.

- I would rather die than speak in front of people.

- If I had to make a living from public speaking I would starve.

I realized a long time ago that not everyone would appreciate or understand my gift, so I learned not to allow those comments to affect me. Be careful not to allow people to project their fears and limitations on you. By giving into those fears, you position yourself to be someone who starts with ability and stops by response. Move forward and see your task to the end. You have what it takes.

- You possess time, talent, and money.

- You are accountable for your time, talent, and money.

- You are in control of your time, talent, and money.

Where would the world be without you? Not the "you" that life has made you, but the "you" who is unique and created to do great works. Your gifts can make the world a better place.

Gifts for Everyone

Gifts are areas of expertise that come naturally to us. It's my belief that those gifts are "wired" in us at birth. Our gifts are the means by which we can make a positive difference in the world. No matter the impact life has on you, the fact remains that you and everyone else for that matter, are in possession of a gift that if properly identified and cultivated into ability, can positively impact the world. Gifts are usually exhibited during childhood. Mozart began to compose at the age of 5. If you are a parent, you may notice the uniqueness of your child. There is a 3 year-old boy whose parents attend my church. Their son loves to talk and he takes every opportunity to speak into a microphone. That is his gift and if properly directed, it could lead

Chapter 3 Your Ability is Valuable

to a wide range of vocations. The types of gifts are limitless, but I've found that our gifts are generally found in one or more of the following areas: mental, physical, social, and spiritual.

Mental

I enjoy watching the faces of participants in my seminars when they hear my motivational speeches or listen to my presentations on stewardship. My gifts to work with numbers, speak to crowds, and write books are examples of a mental gift. These gifts were so powerful that it overrode my college education. Let me explain.

My educational background is in Business Administration, but in high school, a friend convinced me to take an accounting class. I was afraid of accounting because in a movie I had seen, the accountant took the fall when things went bad. In spite of my fears, I was the only person who earned an A in the class, but I dismissed my success, ignored my potential and never took another accounting class.

Although I do not possess a degree in accounting, my aptitude and gift in that area was significant and with commitment, I developed my ability to the point where it helped me become a chief financial officer. As a CFO, I oversaw accounting departments and I helped increase levels of efficiency, effectiveness, and profitability. Mental gifts are talents that you are born with, and develop in life. These talents enable you to increase what is around you through new ideas, problem solving and by providing knowledge to others.

Mental gifts are developed through reading and studying. People with mental gifts are usually very receptive. Therefore, these stewards should dwell in environments suitable for developing their gifts. The effects of excessive distraction have been well documented. Both the quantity and the content of distractions limit the development of mental gifts.

The Growing of You

Mental gifts manifest themselves in several ways. Careers that depend on mental gifts are teachers, lawyers, accountants, financial analysts, scientists, inventors, investors, doctors, business owners, and many others. Imagine if you woke up to a world without your phone. We are so dependent on it, that life without it would be unthinkable. Yet there was a time when it did not exist. Its inventor Alexander Bell changed the world, using his mental gift.

Physical

When I was in high school my friends and I watched an annual NBA slam-dunk contest. Michael Jordan won the competition that year with a dunk from the free-throw line. The prize money exceeded $10,000. Jordan, using a single facet of his physical gift, dazzled the world and increased financially.

Physical gifts are God given and enable you to prosper financially using your body to create things, solve problems, and perform tasks. When you listen to the latest hit songs, watch a movie or television show, you are witnessing the physical gifts of those actors and singers. It is amazing when a professional golfer hits a hole in one, or a singer hits a perfect note or when a bowler scores a perfect 300 game. These people are not superhuman; they are just like you and me. The only difference is that they have developed their physical gifts to an elite level. Those possessing physical gifts develop their skills by practice and repetition. Stewards with physical gifts suffer when they do not practice.

Michael Jordan, one of the greatest basketball players of our time, did not have success in his youth. He didn't even make his high school varsity team his sophomore year. Jordan, however, did not stop practicing. In fact Jordan's consistent practice led to success in the form of six world championships.

Although many of us are unable to leap and dunk from the free-throw line, pitch a perfect baseball game, or bowl a 300, there are other physical gifts that can provide financial success.

Chapter 3 Your Ability is Valuable

You must remember that your physical talent is unique and should not be compared with others. There is an audience for your ability. The world is large enough for Jordan's unique gift and it is large enough for yours. Do not let the success of others stifle your success. Your success starts in your mind.

Mind and Body Connection

I subscribe to the school of thought that the mind and body are one. Whatever affects one affects the other be it positively or negatively.

Eating foods that do not provide sufficient nutrition for the body limits your brain's performance. I learned this the hard way while working on the first draft of this book. During that time, I ate foods that did not contribute to the health of my body. I consumed calories, but not nutrients. During that time, I also stopped exercising and as a result, I gained weight. I was lethargic and it became increasingly difficult to concentrate, which led to inconsistent writing. My knowledge did not change neither did my gift, but the fuel feeding my body was insufficient. As a result, my mental gift was not at peak performance.

To operate a mental gift effectively, you must be free from entanglement. By entanglement I mean free of worries about your clothes, what others think of you and free of what you think of yourself. Entanglement is like a weed that prevents your gifts from growing and bearing fruit. Your mind becomes engaged in areas that you cannot afford to devote energy to. You consider yourself being proactive when in fact, you are reacting to things around you.

Social Friendships

Social friendships can make or break you. Social gifts include the ability to influence, make friends and establish relationships with people. Social gifts will help you navigate social circles in order to meet people who can help you accomplish your life's mission and connect you with people who need your help.

Those in possession of a social gift can have a great influence in the lives of others. A challenge for those with a social gift is the power of the tongue. The tongue is a tool for creation but it can also be a tool for destruction. People naturally gravitate to people who have the ability to use words to encourage or motivate.

Strange as it may seem people also give audience to people whose tongues tear down. Socially gifted people can be prone to manipulation when their gift is exercised through a motive of selfishness. As a motivational speaker, I am aware of the power of the tongue. The words and writings I have shared with others have produced new thriving businesses; encouraged people to go back to school, get out of debt, and pursue their dreams. I have seen peoples' lives transformed for good, and others' lives destroyed simply by words. Socially gifted people must make every effort not to allow slander and gossip to entangle them. Those actions engage the power of the tongue to destroy and divide your energy and focus. Avoid those types of people and be careful to surround yourself with people who can connect you to your destiny.

Spiritual Gifts

Spiritual gifts enable people to minister to the needs of others. I believe this is the greatest gift. To be sensitive to the needs of others amazes me. Everybody is sensitive to their own needs, but to comfort people who are going through difficulties and challenges without entangling yourself with their problems, is an incredible gift.

If you serve others in a humble manner, taking no glory for yourself, then you possess this gift—use it wisely. Spiritual gifted people are servants and as servants, they help people cope with the hurts and pain—past and present. If you are someone who has one of the other areas of gifts (mental, physical or social), but you are not progressing, then you need to connect with someone who has a spiritual gift.

Chapter 3 Your Ability is Valuable

In my adult life, I have been extremely fortunate to have someone who helped me through the pain of a bad relationship and failures. Those events became a barrier to the manifestation of my destiny. Each day I relived those old hurts and sad times; it seemed like no one understood or cared for me. In 1997, I met Dr. Henry L. Porter, a spiritually gifted man, who became my mentor. Dr. Porter helped me sort out those hurts and extrapolate wisdom from those experiences in order to help others. The sincerity of his concern for me tore down the barriers and broke the mental chains holding me back. He helped me see the greater good in the things I experienced so that I could help others through my gift. People in possession of a spiritual gift believe in the power of prayer. Prayer changes things.

Prayer changes the effects of your past, impacts the events of your present, and empowers your future.

Spiritually gifted people believe all things are possible, and that there are no fatal or permanent flaws that can't be overcome with love. Those who love God and spend time reading His Word can expect to have a fruitful relationship with Him.

There are some people, however, who possess a spiritual gift and are more self-serving than they are servants. Their "service" is rooted in pride and a desire to be seen, heard, honored and financially supported by others. They do not possess the mind or heart of a servant that goes with a true spiritual gift.

True spiritually-gifted people are sensitive to the needs of other people. They often feel that it is their responsibility to help people navigate the ups and downs of life.

What You See is What You Get

Working in tandem with your gift is your belief system. Your belief system is your perception of your environment. It's what you believe is true. You and I can look at the same picture, but see different elements of that same picture. Using this example, let's say that someone gives you a pair of rose colored glasses; you don those glasses and immediately your view of the world is rose colored.

Here's the irony of this example, the world did not change, but your perception of the world changed. All too often you focus on changing your circumstances, when the real change needs to be in *you* and how *you* view your circumstances. Perception is your individual reality.

Here is another story to illustrate my point.

Two shoe salesmen Jack and John, who are employed by a multi-national shoe company, are sent to a remote village in Africa. They decide to maximize the territory, so Jack heads south, and John heads north. They agree to meet at a hotel near the airport within seven days. After only a few days of travel into the remote villages, Jack noticed that the villagers did not wear shoes. "How can I sell shoes to people who don't wear any?"

Jack returns to the meeting place earlier than scheduled; he sends a message home saying, "No one here wears shoes, requesting permission to catch an earlier flight to return to America." Jack returns home with his entire inventory. As John travels farther north, he realizes that the villagers do not wear shoes; he takes time to show them the benefit of wearing shoes and sells out his entire inventory. John rushes back to the agreed upon meeting place and sends a message home saying, "No one here wears shoes, requesting more inventory." The story illustrates how your perception of your ability influences your behavior. Both salesmen were in similar situations, but their individual perceptions of their abilities brought about completely different behaviors and different results. If you perceive a situation a certain way, you will act based on your perceived reality. These perceptions and the realities behind them, often do not match. Rarely do we evaluate ourselves based on who we are. So many things we believe about ourselves are not true.

Chapter 3 Your Ability is Valuable

We do not see the whole picture. Just because something happened in your life, does not define your life. Some things in your life happened because you did not know better. Others were simply for the "Growing of You". Whatever the reason, your perception of events will either inspire you to use your abilities for your purpose, or discourage you from using your abilities to meet your purpose. In other words, perception became true for you, even though the event you experienced didn't represent the truth about yourself.

The truth does not change (the villagers do not wear shoes). But, how you perceive the truth (request to come home early, or request more inventory), becomes true for you. The seed for success in any endeavor boils down to: what is true to you; because what is true to you, dictates your actions or inactions. In order to connect with the truth, you must develop a proper belief system, one that sees opportunity and not defeat.

For some of you, the belief system related to your gifts can be summed up in this statement, "I tried something once, but it didn't work, and since it didn't work I won't try it again to spare myself disappointment." It's been said that experience is the best teacher, but what is it teaching you? Your interpretation of that experience can forge how you believe. Did your experience teach you to try something once and draw an unchanging conclusion? Any truly great thing or great person didn't become great in a day. Sometimes you have to try the same thing more than once. I believe that it's life's way of measuring your commitment to your gift. I have had failures and I have measured myself by those failures, which I allowed to stop my progress.

However, I have learned that the measure of success is in what you believe, not what you did. Do you believe that failure equals defeat, or that failure is the first step to success? The number of failures will not hinder your progress unless you believe that those failures define you. Do you believe that you are a gifted person who failed, or a failure with a gift? Do you believe that you can change the world through your gift?

The Growing of You

If you don't, then you will be like the majority of people, afraid to use their abilities and unaware of the potential of their gifts hiding them from the world.

The proper belief system will help you value your abilities and treasure the uniqueness of your gifts. A proper belief system forms a hedge against two obstacles that prevent you from using your gift:

1. Inaccurate valuation of your ability
2. Comparison of your gift with others

It saddens me to see people who are marvelously gifted, but who devalue their ability and who fail to see how they can help others. Even worse is when those same people pronounce that others are "better" than they are. It's not a case of someone being "better", it's simply that those people have five talents, believe in their abilities and operate in areas that are prepared to receive their talents. What should matter is that there is a place for you and your gifts, no matter the number. Each of us has a purpose to fulfill. I have seen fear and doubt make people retreat from life and hide their gift from those who need it and from those who would pay for their help.

Take stock of your life. Is your gift producing measurable results? If not, is your belief system aligned with your mindset? Your mindset is where you want to be, and your belief system is the reason you are where you are. If you are not where you want to be it may time to examine why you are where you are. No one wants to be poor, but all things considered, people remain poor due to their poverty (poor belief system).

Is it possible that the family traditions of the poor form and reinforce belief systems that limit them to poverty? Most people didn't learn about financial matters in school, but learned them from their parents. They may desire a way out of poverty (mindset) but if their belief system promotes consumption over investing and saving then their actions create scenarios based on those beliefs.

Chapter 3 Your Ability is Valuable

Change your mind, change your circumstances. Your gift has the potential to produce, but what hinders production is the belief in some limiting factor that your gift cannot produce.

The Lazy Steward possessed the mindset and training to produce, but his belief system for serving the Master emphasized returning the gold and not increasing it. That's why he chose to hide the money over investing it. The Lazy Steward was given one bag of gold. That gold along with his ability should have produced something. He tells the Master why he did not produce:

"I knew that you are a hard man, harvesting where you have not sown and gathering where you have not scattered seed. So I was afraid and went out and hid your gold in the ground. See, here is what belongs to you."

The Lazy Steward was an investment manager, but he was unable to perceive the Master as an investor, and as such, he became a failure. The Lazy Steward hid his bag of gold in a hole from the world, but eventually, the power and value of that bag of gold manifested through someone with the proper belief system and mindset. In the parable, the Master gave the bag of gold to the steward who possessed 10 bags.

Circumstances did not influence the Lazy Steward and neither did opposition from other people. The main hindrance was his perceptions about the master:

- He was a hard man
- He was a man who harvested where he had not sown

What you perceive is what you believe, and what you believe is what you receive.

The Lazy Steward perceived that the bag of gold was given for him to fail. Same gift, but different perception of it leads to different outcome. This is classic misperception. What he failed to see was that the Master's investment entitled him to an increase. Who gives a bag of gold to a failure? The Lazy Steward's misperception made him suddenly change his vocation from Investment Manager, to "Grave Digger". How does that relate to you?

Misperception can change your purpose and negate your ability rendering it ineffective.

Re-focusing your perception might require a change in how you conduct your life. My grandmother used to say that "birds of a feather flock together", meaning people tend to become like the people they associate with. You may be an "eagle" meant to soar in the sky, but associate with "chickens" pecking in a coop. Even though you are an "eagle" the more often you associate with "chickens" you will begin to think, sound and act like a "chicken". If you spend a great deal of time with people who fail to reach their goals, it's possible that your failure to reach your goals is because you have become drawn into their world and trapped by the gravity of their limitations. Instead of sharing your gift with the world, you adopt habits that hide it. This is not your destiny. Your destiny is to travel to the stars unencumbered by the weight of the world. If you are not on the path to reaching your destiny, then ask yourself why you think, speak and act a certain way. Those reasons are probably limiting your success. Change your perception and experience the joy that comes from having a belief system that gives you energy and strength to pursue your purpose. Your purpose is more than an assignment, it is also empowerment. It will require power to overcome obstacles to see the opportunities beyond them.

Your current experience is not the sum of your life. I am sure that you have been in worse circumstances, but made it through. I remember, with great joy and appreciation, overcoming health issues, financial trials, relationship problems, opposition, and the list goes on, but only when my focus shifted to one central question did I start on the path to victory. I did not ask why things were happening to me; my question was why was I created?

Chapter 3 Your Ability is Valuable

Each time my focus shifted to addressing that question, my problems went from mountains to molehills. It did not happen overnight, but my strength grew each day until I was able to overcome. Focusing on my purpose led me to everything I needed to continue my journey.

Summary

Personal Stewardship is the faithful, prudent and profitable use of one's gifts and talents in line with their ability. Personal Stewardship encourages us to interact with others as we learn to transition from doubting our gifts, to accepting them and using them. The opposition to Personal Stewardship is the deceptive belief that your gift cannot benefit others.

There are three types of opposition that shape your perception and influence your behavior incorrectly, internal opposition, circumstantial opposition and people centered opposition.

There are three keys to the faithful operation of your gifts. Persistence, Patient Endurance and Perseverance.

- Persist when the resistance tries <u>to stop you</u> short of the desired outcome.

- Endure when the desired outcome has not been reached within the timeframe of your efforts and belief system.

- Persevere when the resistance tries to <u>make you stop</u> short of the desired outcome.

Each of us has the potential to prosper through our purpose. The gifts and talents within you are evidence of who you really are. The vehicle by which we unleash that potential is stewardship.

Gifts are areas of expertise that come naturally to us. The types of gifts are limitless, but our gifts are generally found in one or more of the following areas: mental, physical, social, and spiritual.

Your belief system works in tandem with your gift. Your belief system is your perception of your environment and is the reason you are where you are. The proper belief system will help you value your talent and treasure its uniqueness.

Chapter 3 Your Ability is Valuable

Misperception can change your purpose and negate your ability rendering it ineffective.

Focusing your perception on your problems and the problems of others makes them bigger than they are. When you do that, it takes more energy from you and leaves you with less energy to fulfill your purpose. When there is little energy for your purpose, then it's easy to change your purpose according to your perception and not your ability.

Chapter 4
The Power of One: Creation & Development

Creation Starts with You

One of my former classmates asked for my help to motivate his son. The young man was a talented basketball player, but according to his father, he lacked passion to move to the next level. I told the young man that despite what others considered my lack of basketball height, I still managed to dunk a basketball. I told him that people, who were taller than me, taunted and ridiculed me. I told him that I had two choices: either submit to their taunts or commit to developing my talent to the highest degree possible. I chose to develop my talent. Once I committed to making myself better and to focus on my purpose, the taunts stopped and I was accepted as a player.

Once you know your gift and establish a proper belief system, you are prepared to reclaim your birthright. What is that birthright? I call it "The Power of One". There are seven characteristics of humanity that enable us to create and to develop. In order to create, each of these characteristics must operate in unity.

CREATION

1. Imagination: the power to see in the mind's eye.

2. Visualization: the ability to focus on specific things.

3. Goals: the commitment to bring into reality those things seen in the mind's eye.

Chapter 4 The Power of One: Creation and Development

DEVELOPMENT

4. Thoughts: The act or process of thinking.

5. Emotions: the product of your thoughts that motivate your desire.

6. Desire: the power that moves you.

7. Action: the response to desire that brings about the reality you want to create.

Through the "Power of One", people have changed the world. Bill Gates changed the world. The late Steve Jobs changed the world. Oprah Winfrey changed the world. You too can change the world. This list of characteristics seems easy enough. Why do only a few people change the world? What makes these few people different, if we all possess these characteristics? The answer is simple: their lives are dedicated to consistently using the "Power of One" to make a difference. Each person has something that can transform the life of someone. It starts in your imagination, and ends with your actions.

The Good Stewards in the Parable of the Bags of Gold offer examples of the Power of One.

Imagination:
- Good Stewards - Each had the power to increase. The bags of gold are symbolic of imagination. Money that is invested wisely creates money. Imagination is the first step to creation.

Visualization:
- Good Stewards - Each steward visualized an increase in the value of his bags of gold.

Goals:
- Good Stewards - Each committed to bringing his vision into reality.

Thoughts:
- Good Stewards - Each thought about increasing the value of the bags of gold.

Emotions:
- Good Stewards - Each was motivated to desire what he visualized

Desire:
- Good Stewards - Their desire helped them maintain their commitment to increase the Master's investment until he returned.

Action:
- Good Stewards - Their desire moved them to respond in a manner that brought about the reality they wanted to create. By immediately moving to put their money to work, they mixed action with their faith.

In order to bring the unseen into the world of the seen, there must be unity. The unity of imagination, visualization, goals, thoughts, emotions, desire, and action is the power of creation. Here is an example. Years ago, a speaker told me that I could do "business in deep waters". I asked him what that meant and he said that if I took the time to reflect, I would know what he meant. Truth be told, it was not a quick process, but finally this thought came to me: Doing "business in deep waters" meant writing a book. That seemed like an interesting idea, but there were many barriers. After more reflection, I decided to write about stewardship, although at that time I knew nothing about the topic. My inexperience in writing made the process frustrating and there were several times when I wanted to quit, but whenever I took time to reflect and visualize the completed book, I continued to move forward. After consistent visualization, something interesting happened. I wanted to complete the book, more than breathing. This desire inspired me to write on good days, bad days, and even on lazy days. Finally, after about a year of writing, the Power of One produced my book.

Chapter 4 The Power of One: Creation and Development

Imagination

Imagination is a natural ability that enables humanity to create original things. We are the only created beings in possession of this ability. It is the creative process by which mental images go from unseen to seen. What makes imagination so powerful is that we can create anything from our imagination. Race, sex, age, height, weight, or any other physical feature cannot hinder imagination. The Wright brothers imagined that man could fly, Martin Luther King Jr. had a dream of racial equality, and Walt Disney imagined that a mouse could talk.

The number of people who accomplish great things is few because many people have been tricked. Does this sound like you? The pleasures and the limitations from the outside converge to keep you believing that your potential to achieve is based on the state you are in right now. Please hear me clearly, your financial state does not matter; your past failures do not matter; and your physical limitations also do not matter. Your imagination is the most powerful energy source available, more powerful than electricity, more powerful than sunlight, more powerful than radio waves. All of these were harnessed by humanity using the power of imagination.

In today's world, we are inundated with material from all forms of media and as a result, we do not use our imagination. As I said earlier, while writing this book, my imagination waned during a time when I needed it the most. I did not notice it at first, but as time passed, I encountered periods of discouragement and lack of inspiration. My lack of focus became so great that I could no longer see myself achieving my goals. So I prayed, and the answer I received was to imagine.

Excessive television hindered my ability to imagine. The images that I *would* have received were blocked by the constant barrage of someone else's imagination. Any Divine Thoughts that I had could not receive the power from those images, and, it was this lack of power that prevented me from achieving my goals.

The Growing of You

In addition, since I lacked imagination, I began to function on the images presented and became subject to the limitations of those images. During that time, my job became increasingly stressful and like most people when I got home from work, I would plop down in front of the television to relax. After watching a couple of shows, I would try to write, but I could not focus and eventually, I'd go to bed. This pattern repeated itself for months. Not only did I not write anything of significance, but each day I seemed to be wearier.

At the time I was unaware of the effects of television watching on the brain. When you watch television your brain enters alpha mode. In alpha mode your brain is in a passive receptive mode, due to very little eye movement that is required to absorb the images from television. While your brain is in alpha mode, it is susceptible to suggestions, daydreams and the inability to concentrate. Any combination of the three interferes with the focus necessary to use your imagination.

The obvious question is: how do we nurture imagination? Easy...just use it. When was the last time you truly used your imagination I don't mean the part of your imagination that causes you to consider the worst case scenarios. I mean making a conscious effort to imagine something you enjoy, something you see yourself doing, or accomplishing. That power remains inside of you, but it is like a muscle, it gets flabby if you do not use it. Remember when you were a child and you would imagine that you were soaring through space, a queen ruling subjects, or limitless other things.

Start by abstaining from one or more of the following: television, internet, games or music for up to 40 days; use this time to strengthen or enhance your imagination. If you are unable to go 40 days, try shorter increments. In your mind's eye, the focus is on the power of your imagination, not images that are presented to you. Focus on a place in your mind's eye where there are no boundaries or limitations, a place where dreams come true. The more your focus, your imagination becomes material for your vision.

Chapter 4 The Power of One: Creation and Development

Visualization

We live in a world of possibility, but we will not perceive it until we focus. Once you focus, you divert your attention from distraction and set it on things you desire. Once you focus on something specific, your mind will lead you to it. The impossible becomes possible when you focus. That is visualization, the act of using your imagination to create a specific picture of the future supported by your mission in the present. My vision is a world where everyone enjoys their lives by embracing their purpose (through stewardship) without fear or ridicule. In this world everyone uses their abilities and resources to the max and contributes to the lives of others while making the world a better place.

Athletes use visualization to see themselves hitting the mark, reaching the finish line or scoring the winning goal. All these images prompt them to eat, train and give their bodies the proper rest they need to be successful. The more often they see themselves as champions, the easier it is for their bodies to respond in a manner that makes their vision a reality. It can work the same way for you. Your life is a product of vision, yours or someone else's. If you can see it, you can have it. Do you see yourself doing something great?

When I hear people say, "I just can't see myself doing or being that." They are telling the truth. The mind's eye is not open and focused on what is available. However, I want you to open your mind's eye, focus on and move toward your destiny. The way you think blinds your mind, open your eyes by visualizing. Do not get discouraged if you don't see what you want to see with your physical eyes. Use your physical eyes to see what is, and use your mind's eye to see what you want.

You were created for a unique purpose. Within you are gifts, talents, and abilities that are unique to you. The key to an enjoyable and successful life is living with your purpose in mind. Unfortunately, we all face trials, tribulations and setbacks that distract us from our purpose. These trials create so many questions. Why did this happen to me? What did I do to deserve this? How can I get out of the mess I am in? Please understand that in life we do not know all the answers, but we can learn them. Sometimes that learning comes from mistakes made in the past. Learning from the mistake is not possible when you allow the mistake or trial to become the focus, once you do this you lose sight of the vision of your greater purpose.

The Lazy Steward lost sight of his greater purpose. Remember a steward is someone whose responsibility is to direct the affairs of another person; including but not limited to, property and money. Therefore, being a Good Steward was the highest order of his life, because his time, talent and money came from a higher power. The Lazy Steward lost sight of the vision to make himself and the world around him better by exercising his ability to manage and increase his bag of gold. Instead, he chose to focus on the Master, or rather his misperception of the Master. The Lazy Steward said to the Master, "I knew (visualized) that you are a hard man, harvesting where you have not sown and gathering where you have not scattered seed." He focused on the Master being a hard man, and that is exactly what he experienced because his focus prompted him to respond in a way (burying his gold in a hole) that made his vision a reality. The steward's wrong focus caused him to make a choice that took him away from his purpose.

Years ago I experienced a major financial setback due to other people's mistakes. It seemed like there were no opportunities to turn things around. Creditors were calling for money, but I didn't have any. The setback became the defining point in my life, preventing me from moving forward in purpose (circumstantial opposition). For years that mistake haunted me.

My thoughts were besieged by "should" and "could" "I should have done this" or "if I could do it again". My thoughts were focused on the mistake and not the lesson. As long as my focus remained on the mistake, the lesson from the mistake could not propel me to fulfill my mission in life. A mission is the purpose in the present that builds toward the future you envision.

Chapter 4 The Power of One: Creation and Development

Over time I began to direct my focus away from the mistake and then move on in my mission, but I could not. Although I no longer focused on the mistake, I still wanted to punish the people for the hurt they caused me. Each time I saw them, a fury rose inside me that only vengeance could quench. Little did I know, that the more time I spent dwelling on why and how they should be punished, I was drawing their past mistake to the present. Bringing their mistake to the present immobilized me from pursuing my purpose as much or even more than dwelling on my mistake. Just as I deserved the opportunity to learn from my mistakes, they too, deserved the opportunity to learn from their mistakes.

With much soul-searching through prayer, the fury lessened, I was no longer bound by their mistakes. My main challenge became overcoming the fear of what I would become. Would my future look like my past? Was it safer to remain where I was in a cocoon of comfort? My failure led me to fear my potential. I could not bear failing a second time, so I spent time helping others, but I did not help myself. Instead I focused on my failure in order to avoid growing. Are you spending too much time helping other people fulfill their mission and avoiding yours? Be diligent and use your time to forget the past, forgive in the present, and move toward your future.

Goals

Goals are a written representation of what you have visualized. They are a reminder of your commitment to yourself to complete/achieve your purpose and desires. By setting goals based on your main purpose, and other important objectives, you set the tone for selecting tasks that are consistent with your purpose. Goals are a very important component of time management. They ensure that you are doing more than just completing tasks; goals are a constant reminder of where you want to go and they give your mind a picture or destination to focus on. Although a goal may contain a destination, it is much more. A goal is your guide, your strength, and at times your encouragement. People who set goals are usually high achievers, because goals reinforce the importance of visualizing the things you want. There are two misconceptions about goals that hinder people from reaching them:

1. **Goals should be written on paper and forgotten.** Those who do not have goals, do not believe their vision can become real through their actions. If their life changes for good, it is because of some outside force, and conversely, if things do not change, it is because of an unpredictable force influencing their lives. It helps to note that what you visualized is worthwhile. The worthwhile goal keeps you focused on the primary vision because you have many things that randomly distract you. Goals help you turn the vision of the future into reality today.

2. **I have written a goal, but I am discouraged because I do not know what to do.** This misconception comes from not understanding that there are two parts to every goal: Outcome and Performance. Most people are familiar with outcome goals. For example:

- I want to make an A on my math exam next month.
- I want to be married by the time I'm 30.
- I want to be a millionaire by the time I'm 40.

With outcome goals, you define the *what*. Performance goals define the *how*.

These are examples of performance goals:

- I will study algebra three times a week for thirty minutes.
- I will attend one singles gathering a week, and introduce myself to at least five people.
- I will take an investment class next month and save 10% of my monthly income to invest.

Chapter 4 The Power of One: Creation and Development

Here's an example of one of my personal goals.

Physical: Health

Objectives: What you are aiming toward?

My long-term objective is to live to be 125 with no health problems.

My intermediate-term objective is that when I turn 50, to maintain excellent health inside and outside and look and feel younger than my age.

My short-term objective is to avoid diabetes.

Initial weight: 178.5 Target Weight: 168

1. Outcome Goal: I want to lose 15 lbs. of fat, and gain 5 lbs. of muscle within six months.

a. Performance Goal-Action Plan

  i. Cardio Exercise 30 minutes

  (2 times per week)

  ii. Weigh myself

  (Once every two weeks)

  iii. Stretch 30 minutes

  (2 times a week)

  iv. Lift weights

  (2 times a week)

2. Outcome Goal: I want to reduce my resting blood glucose level to 70-100 milligrams per deciliter.

a. Performance Goal-Action Plan
   i. Visit doctor for testing every six months starting in January.
   ii. Eat 150 grams or less of carbohydrates per day
   iii. Get at least 7 hours of sleep.
   iv. Reduce consumption of foods that spike blood sugar
      b. Potatoes
      c. Corn

3. **Reward:** A New Custom Suit

Unbalanced goals can become confusing. Goals are unbalanced when there is an outcome, but no performance. In the example of my physical goal, I listed both outcome and performance goals. When your goals are unbalanced, you become discouraged and you stop pursuing the goals. This leads you to murmuring, complaining, and longing for easier times. You believe that completing your goal is impossible. Longing for the past speaks unbelief to your future. It has been my experience that the proper response to seemingly insurmountable setbacks is to remain focused on your goal, add performance goals to your outcome goals, and review your progress.

No matter how far you think you are from your goal, if it is important to you, then you have probably made some progress toward it. Take that progress and build on it. Use the S.M.A.R.T format to review your goals and to determine their effectiveness.

1. Specific
2. Measurable
3. Attainable
4. Relevant
5. Time-bound

Specific: Your goal should be specific to you. Specific goals generate more interest and enthusiasm for completion. In general, for a goal to be specific consider the following questions:

Chapter 4 The Power of One: Creation and Development

- What: I want to achieve good health
- Why: I want to avoid diabetes and heart problems
- Who: Me and my doctor
- Where: Dinner table and gym
- Which: Give up popcorn and French fries

Measurable: Your goal should be measurable. If your goal is not measurable, you will not be able to determine if you are making progress.

- How much/How many?

I want to lose 15 pounds and gain 5 pounds of muscle

Attainable, Relevant, and Time-bound: Your goals should be attainable and realistic. In order to attain your goals, you might have to stretch beyond your current state, but the process should not become a burden. Consider these questions when considering attainability, relevance and time:

- How can the goal be accomplished?

(Cardio exercises, weight-lifting, stretching, modifying diet). Relevance: Your goal is based on an objective that you are willing and able to work to reach.

- Is this goal worthwhile?

(I want to avoid a diagnosis of diabetes. I want to look and feel younger.) Your goal has a value worthy of your time or effort spent.

- When do I want to accomplish my goal?

(Within six months). Your goal should have a deadline. Setting a deadline helps you to focus on getting the goal accomplished.

Connect your goals, imagination and visualization. The connection enables you to tap into creativity.

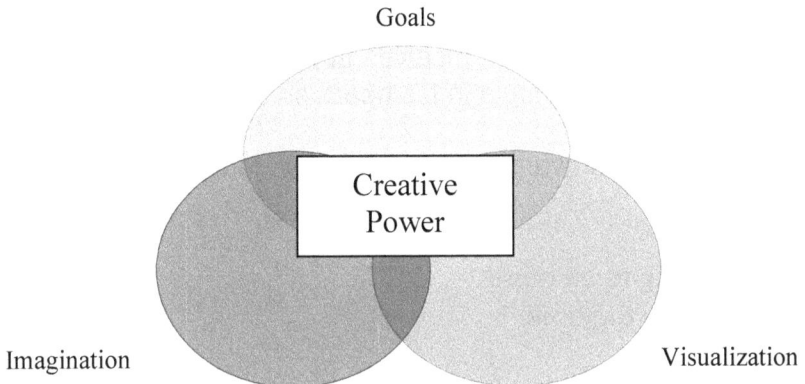

Development Ends Through You

Thoughts

Once you begin to perceive yourself truthfully, there will be a battle between who you once believed yourself to be and the person you are. Although you may have experienced mistakes those experiences do not define you, unless you allow them to. Your past is the result of life experienced independent of the truth. Challenges arise because you erroneously believe that you are the sum of your experiences. When you learn who you are, you must also unlearn what your past says about you.

In other words, learn lessons from all of your failures and disappointments, but they must be forgotten; because your purpose must take precedence in such a way that the press to achieve your goals supersedes your former shortcomings.

Your mind is a powerful tool that can help you reach your goal or stop you from moving forward. Whatever your mind believes is reality—becomes that reality. The question becomes what reality will you believe? Will you believe a reality based on what others have said about you, or will you believe the truth as determined by your purpose?

Chapter 4 The Power of One: Creation and Development

What separates those who experience the reality they were created to live versus those who do not? Stewards who reach their goals understand that there is a universal law that applies to everyone. This law dictates that whatever thoughts dominate your mind, will manifest themselves in your actions. This law is known as, "As a man thinks in his heart, so is he."

Let's say that you want to learn a new language, but your thoughts are:

- This is going to be hard.
- I don't have the time.
- I'm too old.
- I can't afford the software, books, or class.

Your mind, the powerful tool that it is, will create scenarios that will set limits in your life.

There is more to you than what you know. In order to maintain and increase, you must use what you have. If you do not use it, you will lose it. Lose the drive. Lose the opportunity. Lose the idea to someone else. Think about it. If you do not exercise muscles, they will eventually become weaker and smaller. If you do not exercise your memory, you may have a difficult time recalling information. Even money loses its value to inflation, if not used. On the other hand, if you believe that you can *have* what you do not have, then you shall have it.

Belief overcomes opposition. Belief coupled with desire brings results. We have been conditioned to accept the impossible when we live in a world of possibility. Think about it. We can communicate with people around the world with the click of a button; we can send pictures and email from our phones; and we can even shop without leaving our homes. During my childhood, these things were not possible. Except for a few trailblazers and visionaries, these ideas were not common place in the American psyche, but that did not prevent those visionaries from nurturing and bringing their ideas to life.

The Growing of You

What ideas do you have, but do not exist? Just because something does not exist doesn't mean that its creation is impossible. This is where many of you go wrong. You believe that developing your ideas is impossible and as a result, your ideas remain dormant. Your idea might require you to collaborate with someone who possesses a different set of skills or abilities. For example, if you are writing a book, you need an editor, graphics designer, publisher, etc.

Making impossible possible is a higher thought. Divine Thinking from a Divine Being created Divine You for a Divine Purpose. Divine Thinking creates thoughts that go beyond the mundane thoughts of the world. The thoughts of the world are presented via different media, generally television, movies, and music.

When pop culture dominates television, music, and movies repeated exposure can produce like thoughts and attitudes. The results are mediocre people who look for fulfillment through entertainment and who form conclusions based on the opinions and comments of others.

The things you hear, speak, and think are rehearsed in your brain. They become so entrenched in you that you are not aware of the patterns holding you back from your purpose. We are creatures of habit. Once you have established a pattern of doing something, it feels natural, even comfortable.

I once had a fear of public speaking. From ages 10 to 17, I was a sought-after public speaker. It wasn't until an embarrassing situation in college, in which I forgot my lines that fear set in. After that experience, I began to fear what might happen during future speaking engagements. Would I flub my lines, or forget them altogether. My fear became my reality, and once onstage, I sometimes forgot parts of my presentation.

After a few of these embarrassing incidents, I stopped all public speaking. In order to overcome a pattern that had set in, I had to reprogram my thought patterns. For example, each day I had to tell myself that:

Chapter 4 The Power of One: Creation and Development

1. I do not fear public speaking
2. I no longer forget what I have to say when onstage
3. I am a successful, effective and sought-after professional motivational speaker
4. I enjoy public speaking
5. I thoroughly prepare for my speaking engagements

By recording these and similar thoughts on tape and listening to them daily, I began to erase the negative programming from my experience. The first two statements replaced the negative programming, while the final three gave my brain a model to follow. At first, my mind fought this exercise, insisting that all attempts were futile and that this would never work for me.

Based on that one negative experience, my mind was thoroughly convinced that I would forever be a failure as a motivational speaker. After three months, this new programming began to work and I began to change. I summoned enough courage to join Toastmasters, an organization that helps people develop speaking skills and overcome fears about public speaking. Those of you familiar with computers may know the term GIGO (Garbage In, Garbage Out). If your input is garbage, (negativity, doubt, and fear); then your output will be garbage (failure, hesitation). To change your output, you must change your input. The first step is to change your mental programming.

This may require you to stop, or reduce outside programming such as pop-culture found on television, movies, the internet and music. In some cases, you may find it necessary to limit your time around people who subtly program you for failure, or reinforce your mediocrity. The second step is to change your thoughts.

After you have changed your programming, you must begin to absorb thoughts that are positive. After you have done these things, you will begin to develop new thinking patterns. The importance of focused, positive mental programming is illustrated here because without positive programming, mediocre thoughts will influence your new actions, and cause you to delay fulfilling your purpose. You possess mediocre thoughts when you have more excitement and passion for anything other than your purpose. Could you imagine a world where everyone had that level of passion and enthusiasm for their purpose? It would change the world for good.

I am not suggesting that you never watch a television show, see a movie, or listen to music. I am saying that in order to reach your purpose, exercising restraint is required to access Divine Thought. Divine Thought is a thought that elevates you in every way. The more positive, inspirational, and motivational thoughts and concepts you can accept, the greater likelihood you will be able to identify, ignore and break free from negative programming.

Where can you find Divine Thought? It is found in the words—either spoken or written—of those who have changed the world or the world around them. In my life, I have encountered people who planted seeds of positive mental programming in my mind, and the fruit is manifesting itself in my life today. My mother and my maternal grandparents in particular have always been a source of positive inspiration. Whenever I attempted something new, they told me I could accomplish whatever I set my mind to and that they believed in me.

I believed them and whenever I attempt something new, I still hear their voices saying, "We believe in you." That is the thought I have. I believe that anything is possible, if I put my all into it. How is that for positive programming? That simple programming affected my life in childhood and beyond. It is the driving force behind all my successful endeavors. Always remember that your words (written or spoken) are an extension of your thoughts and form the basis for whatever you want to accomplish.

Chapter 4 The Power of One: Creation and Development

Emotions

Emotions are outcome of thoughts. I define emotions as conscious mental reactions that reveal and reinforce existing thoughts. Emotions move you forward, or they can discourage you. Emotions are responses to our thoughts. Emotions are designed to assist our thoughts into becoming reality.

In the parable of the bags of gold, the Lazy Steward presents an example of emotional thinking. The Lazy Steward says, *"Lord, I knew that you are a hard man, harvesting where you have not sown and gathering where you have not scattered seed. So I was afraid and went out and hid your talent in the ground. See, here is what belongs to you."*

The parable does not indicate that the stewards were treated any differently aside from being given bags of gold according to their ability. The Good Stewards were able to focus on their purpose, but the Lazy Steward's unresolved emotions, to a past event, adversely influenced his performance. In fact, his repeating the matter to the Master is evidence that his emotions reinforced his thinking into action that hindered his progress.

Are your emotions hindering you? If so, it means your thinking is not aligned with your goals, or your purpose. For example, let's say that you have a problem with weight. You eat and overeat which brings temporary satisfaction, but in the end this causes you to feel sad and depressed.

You feel like you can't get a handle on your weight and you feel like a failure. In this example, your emotions are holding you on the point of your weight. The importance of being aware of your emotions is to trace them back to the root cause and correct your thinking. Make it a practice to evaluate your emotions in order to avoid reactions based on negative emotions that don't line up with your purpose. Aligning your emotions with your purpose gives you energy and a sense of joy to pursue your purpose. Emotions are the seed that motivate you to desire action or inaction.

Desires

To desire is to long for; to wish for earnestly; to covet. Have you ever desired something and that desire was more powerful than a want? Did you receive it? Most likely you did, because your desire is fueled by your emotions. Desire is the fruit of the seeds of emotion. Emotions build up desires within you to act or respond in a certain way. What you desire is satisfaction from fulfilling your purpose. Misplaced desires (prioritizing things over purpose) bring about the opposite effect, causing you to go through life feeling unfulfilled.

Misplaced desires do not bring lasting satisfaction. That is why that new car, new phone, new this or that will bring only temporary and limited satisfaction. Now, I don't mean that you should not enjoy things or life, but when you put pleasurable pursuits ahead of purpose, you forfeit long-lasting satisfaction.

You must educate your desires with the proper imagination, visions, goals, thoughts, and emotion. If you don't, then you will allow almost anything to invade your thoughts and influence our emotion. Misplaced desire can lead you to act contrary to who you are.

To understand desire in action, the parable of the bags of gold provides an example. Each steward possessed the ability to increase the value of the bags of gold entrusted to him. Each Good Steward's desire was to manage and increase what his Master had given him, as evidenced by their actions (i.e. doubling the value of the original bags of gold). The Lazy Steward's only desire was to give the Master back his original investment. He said, "Lord, I knew that you are a hard man, harvesting where you have not sown and gathering where you have not scattered seed. So I was afraid and went out and hid your talent in the ground. *See, here is what belongs to you."*

We see that the Lazy Steward was afraid of the Master, and that fear prompted him to desire to return what belonged to the Master, unchanged. The Lazy Steward had a poor belief system.

Chapter 4 The Power of One: Creation and Development

The components of a poor belief system are negative thoughts, emotions, desires and actions. It was the Lazy Steward's perception of the Master that caused him to experience the emotion of fear.

This emotional experience led him to return what the Master had given him. Desire forces you to act even if that action is inaction. Desire is the motivation that inspires you to act. That is why it is important that your thoughts, imagination, visions, goals and emotions are aligned in order to fulfill your purpose. When they are, your desire will lead you to do and or maintain the actions needed to produce or accomplish whatever you desired.

The Good Stewards desired to fulfill their purpose and that led to rulership, riches and honor. Simply desire to be the best you can be. Seeking purpose changes you. The Good Stewards were changed into rulers as a byproduct of their desire to find and follow their purpose. If you satisfy purpose, it will satisfy you.

Actions

What separates a Good Steward from a Lazy Steward is the response to opportunity. Opportunities are all around us. Life plays no favorites. No one person is "luckier" than another. The person who seems lucky simply perceives, believes, desires, and responds appropriately to opportunity.

We act on the beliefs and desires that are inside us, but our desires can be influenced by misperception. Each steward received at least one bag of gold. They all possessed the ability to manage and increase at least one bag of gold, but one did not respond according to his ability. Your desires are manifested through your actions or inaction. There are three types of actions in stewardship:

- Non-Active Response
- Passive Response
- Active Response

Non-Active Response

Once the Lazy Steward got his bag, he buried it. He did not manage or increase the value of his gold, eventually losing what he had. This is an example of Non-Active Response. It's a moving away from who you really are and what you are capable of doing. Those who practice non-active response allow other forces (fear, unresolved emotions) to dictate their actions or inactions.

I'm reminded of the time when I allowed the unresolved emotion from a business loss and failure to dictate my future actions. For years, I was aware of my ability to speak words of encouragement into the lives of other people, but the unresolved emotion from that event became my reference point. New and exciting opportunities in the area of motivational speaking were filtered through my unresolved emotions. Instead of pursuing those opportunities, I moved away from who I was and remained in a place that seemed comfortable, but in fact was detrimental to my future and my ability to help others. Words from my trusted friend Henry, inspired me to face those unresolved emotions head on in order to move beyond them.

Passive Response

A passive response acknowledges the importance of an active response, but as a result of fear, or a lack of confidence, produces only the minimum response.

A passive response keeps <u>you</u> from losing what you have, but it does not create gain while using your full ability. The Master advised the Lazy Steward of this response when he said, *"You wicked, lazy servant! So you knew that I harvest where I have not sown and gather where I have not scattered seed? Well then, you should <u>have put my money on deposit with the bankers, so that when I returned I would have received it back with interest.</u>"*

Chapter 4 The Power of One: Creation and Development

The Master believed that the Lazy Steward's fear of being held accountable should have prompted an appropriate response. That response was to deposit the money with the bankers, and receive interest. In today's context, that means we should volunteer our gifts to help organizations and people in need. People who lack certain gifts understand the value of your gift even if you don't feel comfortable with your level of ability. Does it matter if you only type 30 words per minute, when someone who can't type needs a typist? The "interest" we would receive in our lives is twofold.

First, we receive a sense of satisfaction from helping other people, and second, we can develop our confidence in our gifts. This is the minimum response for the bearer of gifts.

Active Response

Active Response is where confidence in yourself and the understanding of what you can do inspires action toward accomplishing your purpose. It doesn't matter what you start with, or where you start, simply start. The longer you delay, the greater the chance you will descend into a passive or worse- non-active response.

Both of the Good Stewards started with a different number of bags of gold. What they shared in common was inspired action and confidence in themselves to use what they had to pursue their purpose. Their success didn't lie in the amount of money they possessed. The outcome of their efforts was the same, double the original investment. The power to succeed was in them, as it is in you.

The greatest hindrance to your success is a reluctance to start. Understand that there are people who need help from someone with your unique gifts and ability. Don't sit and wait for them. They have a need but may not recognize you as the solution. Take what you have and begin the pursuit of your purpose. Your purpose is to meet the world's need to an extent that in meeting their needs you develop value that results in increase for you. Anybody or anything that pushes you back to old habits once you have set out to pursue your purpose is not a part of your life.

Describe Your Talent

We all have talents. What separates the person who successfully uses those talents, and the person who does not, is belief. By believing in your talent, you accept that:

1. Your talent is unique.
2. Your talent is valuable.

Your Talent is Unique

In all occupations, there are successful people. There are some who are successful actors, singers, models, teachers, doctors, etc. What contributes to the success of these individuals? Their unique talent contributes to their success. Each successful person who has learned to believe in the uniqueness of his or her talent has discovered a key ingredient to success.

People who believe in their unique talents do not limit their talents or themselves. The servant who was given two bags of gold did not complain that he did not have five. He believed in the uniqueness of his gift and as a result doubled his bags of gold. The lazy servant, however, did not believe in his unique talent, and was paralyzed with fear and suffered loss.

How many of you are paralyzed with fear and discouragement, because you do not sing like Celine Dion, dunk like Michael Jordan, write like the late Maya Angelou, or speak like the late Zig Ziglar? Most of us have been taught that if you cannot be No. 1, then being No. 2 is not worth the effort. The secret to success is not who is No. 1, but it means going as far as your talent will take you. We need a paradigm shift to stop viewing uniqueness as a weakness; we need to claim it as a strength.

Chapter 4 The Power of One: Creation and Development

Your Talent is Valuable

I had a job where the supervisor devalued my talent by saying that without a master's degree I would be unable to secure a job that paid more than I made at the time. Despite his prediction, I received two promotions in two years, and I helped the company make millions. Unfortunately, I did not think enough of myself to leave. I was satisfied making bread for others and eating crumbs for myself. The supervisor was right in a sense, because my value exceeded what that job paid. When I did leave, my earnings soared. After that, I understood my value. Whether or not you have a job, this is recession-proof wisdom. Once you understand your unique value, you set yourself up for promotions and or pay raises, no matter the job.

Deliver Your Talent

Before my practice grew, I often spent time lamenting that I did not have clients knocking down my door. Later, I realized that I had not moved past *interest* in operating a business to being committed to operating a business. Interested people do not put their whole heart, money, and time into their business, committed people do. People had a need for financial consulting, but printing thousands of business cards and leaving them in boxes was not the answer. I needed to identify my services, develop them, and take what I had to offer to the marketplace. The marketplace is where people can benefit from your gift. Having the best product or greatest talent does nothing for you if it is not in the marketplace. The Lazy Steward discovered this firsthand. Because he hid from the market, the results were: no increase. No one else knew that he had the talent, because he buried it in the ground. The other stewards immediately went to the marketplace and it responded in kind. There is a principle here: to receive from the market, you must let the market know what you have to offer. Now, I am not suggesting that if you have a talent that you jump into a business without developing the level of competence that the marketplace demands. Each Good Steward possessed ability (competence) and took that to the appropriate marketplace.

Summary

There are seven characteristics of humanity that enable us to create and to develop. In order to create, each of these characteristics must operate in unity.

CREATION STARTS WITH YOU
1. Imagination
2. Visualization
3. Goals

DEVELOPMENT ENDS THROUGH YOU
4. Thoughts
5. Emotions
6. Desire
7. Action

No one person is "luckier" than another. The person who seems lucky simply perceives, believes, desires, and responds appropriately to opportunity. Your desires are manifested through your actions or inaction. There are three types of actions in stewardship:

- Non-Active Response
- Passive Response
- Active Response

We all have talents. What separates the person who successfully uses those talents, and the person who does not, is belief. By believing in your talent, you accept that:

1. Your talent is unique.
2. Your talent is valuable.

Chapter 5
Your Money is Valuable

Acknowledge – money not yours
Accept responsibility - management of it
Affirm - to increase it
Act - to enjoy and share it with the world

Turning Your Sense into Dollars

Financial Stewardship is the faithful, prudent and profitable use of your money. Understanding how to manage and increase money creates options. Wise pursuit of those options can help develop the connectedness between what we have and what others need. We can use this connectedness to change the world by investing, saving, spending, and giving.

Generating and maintaining wealth is a process that requires spending with frugality, sharing with generosity, and investing creatively. These three core principles are all part of a larger system of financial management. Follow these core principles in order to be an effective Financial Steward.

- Frugality
- Generosity
- Creativity

Frugality

During the real estate boom some homeowners took out second, and in some cases, third mortgages in an attempt to satisfy their desire (or longing) for material things. Spending was the prevailing thought and the "good" times seemed like they would never end, but they did. Unemployment began to rise, access to credit dried up, and housing values plummeted.

One of the most important lessons learned from those times is frugality. Frugality does not mean penny pinching. Frugality is the discipline of spending without waste. Your money has a purpose beyond pleasure, but that doesn't mean you shouldn't use some of your money for pleasure. I have close friends who have traveled to exotic places all over the world. Yet despite their journeys, they manage to be frugal. They maintain flexible schedules that allow for last-minute travel deals that save them hundreds, if not thousands of dollars.

Being frugal brings control (how you spend) over an uncontrollable situation (the economy). Costs are often uncontrollable, but how much you spend is within your control. *"Waste not; want not"* the old saying goes.

Wise spending ensures that you do not waste money on items that cost too much to purchase, maintain and insure. If you can get in the habit of not wasting money, you will decrease your chances of want in lean times.

In order to be a good financial steward, frugality is necessary. Learn the difference between necessity and discretionary spending. Food is important and necessary, but is it necessary to eat out five nights a week? Clothing is important and necessary, but is it necessary to buy the most expensive outfits every month? Try to wean yourself from spending luxuries, one at a time. Instead of going out to dinner five nights a week, try going out just two nights. Excessive spending brought about the problem and it will take disciplined spending, to solve it. To achieve wealth, you must change habits that create waste. Einstein said, *"Insanity is doing the same thing over and over again and expecting different results."*

Generosity

When a man gives freely, he gains because giving creates opportunities to gain. Please allow me to illustrate. Early one morning while on my way to the ATM to deposit two $100 bills, I saw a man walking through the parking lot.

Chapter 5 Your Money is Valuable

He had a brown bag lunch and he looked as if he was on his way to work. He was dressed plainly, but something about him inspired me to give him one of the $100 bills.

Now, I admit, at first I said to myself, "What are you thinking?" You need to make that deposit; you do not even know that man. So, I got in my car and headed to the bank, but before I got there, I decided to follow my unction. By some miracle, I caught up with the man who was outside of a convenience store. I walked up to him and said, "Sir, I believe that I'm supposed to give you this $100 bill. He looked at me with astonishment and started to smile. The man said he was headed downtown to find day labor work, and that while he was walking he prayed for help to pay his bills. He thanked me and I encouraged him to keep praying.

Your generosity can be the answer to someone's prayer and an answer to your own prayers. Your generosity can refresh others who are burdened by seemingly unsolvable problems. People with insufficient resources are encouraged by your kindness. The sincerity of your involvement in their life does more than meet their needs; it gives them hope beyond their resources. Have you ever been in a situation where your resources were insufficient? We have all been there, and it makes our heart sick. But, do you remember the joy you had when someone gave you an unexpected gift, or paid a bill for you? I'm touched by stories on the internet like thousand dollar tips given to servers working their way through school. We all desire to matter, and what better way to matter than in the life of someone in need? Their appreciation and joy refreshes your soul. Even witnessing the generosity of others refreshes your soul.

Generosity is a willingness to give or share unselfishly without expecting anything in return. What makes generosity so amazing is that even though there is no expectation of return, that's exactly what you get. It's about touching the lives of people but results in abundance touching your life.

In the example above would you believe that a few days later, I received more money unexpectedly than I had given that man? Though I was pleased by the financial increase, my desire was to be an agent of hope enabled by the abundance I received to live a prosperous life and touch the lives of people.

You do not have to be wealthy to be generous, but generosity increases your ability to gain. Generosity is one of the pillars of increase. People tend to view increase as one way: flowing toward them. This viewpoint of increase can lead to selfishness and lack of empathy. Sure, there are some people who may take advantage of your kindness, but does that mean you should no longer generous in the belief that it will preserve your wealth? Increase flows in both directions: to you from others; and from others to you. A willingness to give is also a willingness to receive.

Be generous without:

- **Expectation of return.** If you expect something in return, the money becomes a transaction instead of a gift. Money given in secret is rewarded openly.

- **Compulsion.** If you are compelled to be generous you are giving with an open hand, but a closed heart. A closed heart is unwilling to give and unable to receive.

- **Hurting yourself financially.** If your altruism prompts you to be generous at the expense of your own financial stability, you have created a need for yourself. Generosity does not require you to give all.

Creativity

Within you lies the power to gain wealth. The nature of that power is found in your talents and gifts that create a means to bring about wealth. That wealth is manifested through your creativity. Creativity is the creation of something new.

Chapter 5 Your Money is Valuable

The world is always looking for something new, and is willing to exchange money for a new product or service. When I was in high school, there were no iPhones, iPads, Facebook, Twitter, Yahoo or Google, but through entrepreneurial creativity, the creators of those products have become billionaires. Successful products are not created because you simply have an idea. Neither is wealth created because you have money. A willing effort must be made to increase wealth. Embracing inspiration is the catalyst for that effort.

In the parable of the bags of gold, the Master was the inspiration for each steward to manifest his creativity through the creation of wealth. Each steward possessed the ability to create wealth in proportion to the number of bags in his possession. The Master knew each of their abilities and gave them the appropriate number of bags according to their talents. The Good Stewards, through their creativity, put their gold to work and were able to double their gold. Their success is the result of inspiration, effort, and creativity working together.

Today, we also rely on inspiration to create wealth. Is homeownership your inspiration, or maybe starting your own business? My inspiration is the trust my creator has in me to create. No matter the source of inspiration, it prompts you to create a life beyond where you are now, and higher than you have been. Creativity requires effort to create something new, but inspiration is the catalyst behind that effort.

We all have access to inspiration, but some people fail to connect to inspiration due to laziness. Laziness is the refusal to exert the effort needed to create — despite possessing the ability to do so. Laziness limits you; causes you to remain the same.

A lazy and uninspired life avoids creation, hides who you are and what you are capable of achieving. The catalyst behind laziness is the replacement of inspiration with an attitude of fear, pain, tiredness, and being overwhelmed. In the parable of the bags of gold, the Lazy Steward failed to create because he was afraid of the Master.

The Growing of You

He also expressed a feeling of being overwhelmed when he told the Master that he was a hard man, harvesting where he had not sown and gathering where he had not scattered seed. The attitude of fear and perception that he was too overwhelmed to complete the task became more influential than the inspiration for completing the task. These were symptoms of why he didn't create wealth, but the larger problem was that he did not have a relationship with the source of his inspiration (the Master).

Examine the nature of your relationships. Are you spending more time listening to the problems of other people? No successful person accomplished great achievements burdened by the problems of other people. No wonder you lack inspiration, because the people you relate to the most, are people who consistently fail to connect with inspiration to create, and they subtlety train you to live that way as well. They see no reason to exert effort to reach their potential and find it easier to remain the same. Who do you know that is a source of inspiration to motivate you, and hold you accountable? Connect with them, and you will see your creativity rise.

Spend Yourself Out of Debt

When money is entrusted into your hands, you are to spend it in such a manner, that there is no threat of loss from spending; there is a reduction of debt; and there is an increase in savings.

Spending

What is spending? Spending is defined as paying out or using up money. While everyone spends, not everyone spends in the same way or for the same reasons.

Spending habits can either be stepping stones to prosperity or they can lead to financial ruin. Some people spend as a way to find emotional satisfaction while others spend as a way to feel powerful. Spending is relative to the individual.

Chapter 5 Your Money is Valuable

But spending becomes a problem when the items and lifestyle you purchase (desire) become more important than your journey to financial stability and independence. We all spend, therefore our focus and goal, should be to eliminate or change bad habits associated with spending. The most damaging spending habits are:

- Impulse buying
- Overspending

For every cause, there is an effect. If your spending is based on bad habits (impulse buying, overspending, etc.), you will eventually realize the effect of such actions (debt, financial disarray and instability, etc.).

Spending is not a problem, but becomes a problem when it is out of control. Remember, the real objective of having money is control. Any control lost in one area of your finances has a ripple effect in others. If you decide to spend more than you earn, your other financial categories (savings, giving, investing and paying debt) will suffer.

Bad habits do not develop on their own, they are encouraged by a catalyst. My experience has taught me that there are five ways bad spending habits can lead to out-of-control spending.

1. Advertising
2. Expectations of Others
3. Love of Pleasure
4. Depression
5. Lack of Sound Financial Management

Advertising

Advertising is the seed (or root) of overspending. Advertisers attempt to convince consumers that their product will meet a need. In chapter four, I discussed the television-induced "hypnotic effect" called the alpha mode.

Alpha mode greatly reduces your mind's capacity to think. It also greatly enhances your susceptibility to suggestions. Once planted, images are difficult to remove. This explains why you might have difficulty remembering your spouse's birthday, but you can remember the jingle from a 20 year old commercial. A.C. Nielsen Company reports that by the age of 65 the average person has seen 2 million commercials. Advertising's ability to plant suggestions in your mind is a leading factor in the purchase of consumer products that you were enticed into believing you needed. You did not know that you "needed" a new car until a television commercial told you to ditch your old ride.

Advertising alone has the potential to destroy your personal budget and when coupled with messages about marketing and lifestyle, the potential to overspend can become a way of life. Lifestyle marketing is marketing a product that appeals to a person's activities, interests and attitudes. Keep this in mind, advertisers would not spend millions on advertising and product endorsers, if the returns on their investment were not greater than the cost.

Once an advertiser connects a product to you, you are sold. For example, if you believe that a celebrity wears a certain brand of shoes, you will get those shoes, no matter the cost. Credit card commercials are notorious for projecting a lifestyle that most people cannot afford, or that can only be achieved through the frequent use of consumer credit. Embracing this lifestyle makes us vulnerable to the expectations of others and the love of pleasure.

Expectations of Others

The expectations of others can lead to anxiety, worry, and overspending, especially during the holiday season. Millions of people sink deeper into debt as a result of the expectations of others. Commercials are notorious for inducing guilt and creating expectations.

Chapter 5 Your Money is Valuable

For example, Valentine's Day is a bonanza for jewelry merchants. They project the illusion that in order to be a good partner, you must buy your significant other a gift (preferably diamonds). I experienced this with my wife. During our engagement, I was in the process of purchasing a home and every penny was precious; however, I felt extreme pressure from others (not her) to purchase an expensive diamond engagement ring. Finally, when I could take no more, I spoke with my fiancée and explained that buying a home would set us on the path to generating wealth. I could always buy an engagement ring later. Fortunately she understood, and I was able to proceed with purchasing the home.

Love of Pleasure

The love of pleasure is an insatiable desire for pleasure. A tangible expression of the Love of Pleasure is the Love of Possessions (e.g. cars, homes, jewelry). The love of pleasure (the love of possessions) seldom offers long-lasting satisfaction or fulfillment. The desire for more pleasure and new possessions, with no regard for cost, can lead to excessive spending.

Media that heighten the desire for, and expectation of, pleasure constantly bombard us. As you indulge in these pleasures (excessive television, games, movies, etc.), there is a good chance that you will become undisciplined and lazy.

As discipline decreases, so does the ability to control your money and to generate finances. Those who love pleasure more than prosperity, have a greater propensity to poverty because they end up paying more for services (e.g. premium cable channels, games, entertainment, gadgets, electronics, etc.), and fail to increase their savings. When the enjoyment of things is not paired with discipline, there are no spending limits and eventually, no money. As the Proverb indicates, *"He that loves pleasure shall be a poor man."*

Depression

This psychological state is a known instigator for overspending. There are some of you who may view spending as a therapeutic distraction especially when your spirits are low. Spending should not be used to treat this condition. There may also be instances when a lack of money draws a person into depression. Then, there is the possibility that the lack of sound financial management is the true culprit. In all instances, it is best to seek professional help.

Lack of Sound Financial Management

This deficiency affects people who focus primarily on generating money, and not on developing the ability to make money work (management). Freedom from financial woes by unexpected wealth, will not solve your problems. Money is a faithful and obedient servant, but a poor master. If you do not manage your money, it will manage you. Your inability to manage money will continue to enslave you and keep you bound until you learn strategies and methods that will cause you to increase and maintain your finances.

Identify Hindrances to Spending Correctly

For people to prosper and for their money to grow, it must be used from a position of control. That is, you control it by having it work for you. Money is not likely to flourish when it is possessed by a person who is hampered by the following:

- Worry
- Lack of financial control
- Love of pleasure

If you pay attention to the circumstances of your life, you give up control of your time, talent and money. As you yield control, you lack a sense of direction, because you are pulled from circumstance to circumstance. All of your energies are devoted to addressing circumstances and not to achieving your goals.

Chapter 5 Your Money is Valuable

For example, imagine a circumstance where you do not have money to pay your mortgage and the bank eventually forecloses. If you worry that you may lose your home to the point that it consumes your thoughts, it short-circuits your power and ability to generate money and pursue options that may prevent the foreclosure. The things you worry about create a barrier to the solution to your problems. Money cannot flow when you are worried about foreclosure. Worry restricts your money's flow and can cause you to spend money in order to make yourself feel better about your situation – which causes money to become your master.

If you lack financial control over your money, it will not grow, because your money becomes a tool of your circumstance. The main goal of a "pleasure seeker" is to escape reality. An escape from reality is a means for avoiding the responsibilities of life, which includes sound money management. Pleasure seekers relinquish control of their money for the "high" of pleasure. It breaks my heart when I see people who, after exhausting their resources, turn to debt to continue the "high" of pleasure, unaware how this addiction causes them to spiral into unbearable debt and poverty.

Spending Wisely

Learning to spend wisely is a major step in becoming a good financial steward. Once you learn how to spend wisely, you maintain control over your money. It is essential that you learn how to:

1. Spend based on what is best for you. The basis of control is your personal values and goals. Spending your money based on what everyone else buys, wears or possesses can distract you from reaching your goal. A general rule of thumb is to let a day or two pass before you make a major purchase. Give yourself time to see if the impulse (desire) to purchase is still present.

2. Spending does not become a problem until it is out of control. Impulse spending is a distraction from your values and goals. Change your spending habits by eliminating impulse buying. Make a list of the things you need; clip coupons for savings. Set a spending limit in accordance with your financial plan. When possible, research and compare prices on big-ticket items and negotiate for the best price.

3. Spend with your financial plan in mind. There are two ways of getting what you want: the right way and the wrong way. For example, if you want to take a vacation that costs $1,000, and you are already in debt, putting that vacation on your credit card is the wrong way to get what you want. Saving for the vacation and seeing it as a goal, is the right way to get what you want. Making purchases the wrong way tears you down (bad habits, debt, etc.) and doing it, the right way builds you up (setting goals and achieving them).

If you do not want debt, do not borrow. If you do not want to go deeper into debt, do not borrow. Armed with the knowledge of your spending habits, you can develop a budget and reverse your descent into debt. Ninety percent of personal bankruptcies result from credit card abuse or unforeseen expenses.

Your car is going to require repairs. Set aside money for those repairs now. A budget helps you anticipate unplanned expenditures that often end up on a credit card, which creates more debt. Spending the correct way will move you from wishful planning to saving money, and into a specific plan of action.

The word "debt" causes anxiety and worry in many people. No one wants to have and to hold consumer debt, but people find ways to acquire it through the use of credit cards or consumer financing.

Chapter 5 Your Money is Valuable

Every Christmas, no matter the state of their personal finances, fathers, mothers, grandparents, aunts and uncles, spouses, etc., try to give their loved ones a "good Christmas." They end up buying gifts that they cannot afford and then they are stuck dealing with the consumer debt woes in January and beyond.

Consumer debt keeps your financial focus on the past. The outcome of consumer debt is that the money due in the future will be more than the value of the original purchase. For example, if you purchase an I-Pad in December on credit for $600, and you take two years to pay it off, by the time you add on interest, you have forked over far more than the original purchase price of $600. If you need to finance that I-Pad, then you really cannot afford it. Again, think about the interest being added to the repayment of the principal. As you engage in more transactions of this nature, eventually your finances will be unable to support the required payments.

Judging by the number of people in debt, this inability to understand consumer financing leads to a lack of money. Consumer debt is the result of out of control spending. That makes it a type of slavery because the borrower is slave of the lender. Although human slavery is illegal in America, economic slavery exists and many people are enslaved by the economics of their life.

Some of you may be saying, "What is the big deal?" I pay off my credit card bill each month. Good for you, but consumer debt is a master and *that* master can keep you from being creative with your money. Debt is a distraction from your purpose, and it stifles creativity. If you do not understand that the proper use of money can create money, then your enslavement to debt will create money for someone else.

To gain a greater understanding of the effects of consumer debt, let us look more closely at five characteristics shared by debt and slavery.

The Growing of You

1. Both can prevent you from doing the things you want to do (living debt free; having an abundant life).

2. Both can lead to poor health.

3. Both can breed anxiety, despair, depression, distress, bitterness, worry, and discontent.

4. Both give someone else power over you, until you take steps to remove the things (debt) that hinder you.

5. Both can force you into hard labor.

What prevents you from doing what you would like to do? Do you feel like you cannot do anything or go any place until you pay off old debts? Indebtedness causes you to work harder. The lender will require that you work hard in order to repay him. This prevents you from thinking about what you really want to do with your money.

Negative emotions and stress can adversely affect your mind, and whatever affects your mind, manifests itself in your body. The mind and body are two sides of the same coin. High blood pressure, cardiovascular problems, arthritis, etc., are physical manifestations of the effect of negative emotions and stress on the mind. These emotions cause you to feel miserable when you can't do what you want to do.

Negative emotions will cause you to worry and become stressed when your debt payments exceed your income. This leaves no other clear option other than to labor for another's profit. The harder you work, the richer the lender becomes. Consumer debt may result from any, or a combination, of several factors:

- Lack of financial management
- Lack of saving
- Lack of understanding debt
- Lack of willingness to delay gratification

Chapter 5 Your Money is Valuable

Lack of Financial Management

The lack of financial management may cause you to be unaware of the state of your finances. This is understandable because most people have not been taught financial management. As a result acquisition of things becomes more important than saving and increasing wealth. This lack of financial management has been passed from generation to generation, resulting in consumers who purchase things (cars, clothes, jewelry, etc.) they cannot afford.

Lack of Saving

We all experience troubles in life, but some suffer more from those storms because they have not saved for unexpected events. They cannot see beyond today in order to develop the discipline to live in prosperity tomorrow.

Lack of Understanding Debt

We live in a time in which we can acquire almost anything we want by credit; however, accessibility comes with a price, known as interest. Interest means an extra amount of money paid, above what is borrowed. Things purchased on credit extend many people beyond their financial means, and interest increases the creditor's investment at the borrower's (your) expense.

Lack of Willingness to Delay Gratification

Do you know someone who has a new outfit or a new gadget every month, but always wants to borrow money from you to pay their mortgage, rent, gas or cell phone bills? That person's undisciplined desires (unwillingness to save for what he or she wants) continually leads to debt. Do not lend this person money. Do not let your financial goals and plans suffer because that person lacks financial discipline.

How to Stay in Debt

If you continue to spend money or use credit for temporary pleasures, you will create an unending cycle of servitude to the lender. Indulgence only temporarily makes you forget reality. As with slavery, you can seek to escape debt by running away (ignoring it), but when you get caught, you will pay the consequences. Those consequences can include legal judgments, poor credit scores, and reduced spending power, etc.

There are people who are unfazed or indifferent to things such as credit scores and how it impacts their financial future. For those people, their inability to see beyond their current desires severely limits their financial prosperity. I am sure there are a number of you reading this book who were born into a family of debtors, beginning with your grandparents, parents, aunts, uncles, cousins and so on. Does this sound like you? Are you convinced that you are destined to a life of debt? Have you become numb or have you armed yourself with indifference to debt instead of seeking treatment? As with any negative condition, if left untreated it could have catastrophic results.

As the conditions worsens, people start to look for gimmicks or quick fixes such as a rich uncle, or they play the lottery, or they wait for one of those sweepstake clearinghouses to call, or some even dream that an armored truck may accidentally leave one bag of money at their doorstep.

A windfall of money does not guarantee freedom from debt. A lack of money is not always the cause of debt, financial ignorance can lead to debt. So, if financial ignorance causes debt, then financial wisdom is needed to eliminate debt. Having an abundance of money would only make the situation worse. So often I encounter people who say they are praying for money to satisfy debts, but they have never attended a financial seminar, mine or anyone else's. By praying for money, they are asking for an intervention to address the symptom, but not the root cause of their problem.

Chapter 5 Your Money is Valuable

I am sure that you have heard stories of people who have come into large sums of money. Conventional wisdom suggests that they would eliminate their debts and live happily ever after, but this is not always the case. These people take on more debt and in some cases, it exceeds the amount of money they acquired!

People who are a little more practical believe that hard work will help them eliminate debt. This is not always the case especially if the hard work keeps you from developing the gift that will prosper you. Early in our marriage, my wife wanted to get a part-time job to earn extra money and to liquidate some of her debts. I suggested that she not take on this additional work solely for money. Here's why: I told her that for the amount of time required to travel to the job, the vehicle expense, the additional stress, the increase in taxes (remember, "the more you make, the more they take"), and the low pay, I could see no discernible benefit to her. The job was not related to her goals, objectives, or training. The second job would have kept her from working on the gift in which she is truly talented, which is writing. As any serious writer knows, writing requires time and dedication. Working 18 to 24 extra hours a week would seriously hamper her writing and her future success. Which is more beneficial: working hard on a job for short-term cash, or working on your talent for long-term prosperity? She decided to heed my advice and the debts she wanted to liquidate were paid, the book she wanted to write is complete, and the things she wanted to buy were purchased debt-free.

Finally, consolidation loans are a last-resort debt stopgap and definitely should not be considered before developing a solid understanding of how debt works. When you consolidate debt, you are trading short-term obligations for long-term debt. While it is possible your monthly payments could be lower, the total amount of debt you owe increases. By not addressing the cause of debt (financial ignorance) or at the very least, reducing or stopping credit card spending, people eventually allow their habits to pull them into an even worse financial position.

The Growing of You

Keep in mind that you need more than a respite (rest) from debt. Your ultimate goal is to be free. Your decision to not borrow your way out of debt is a step in the right direction. All consolidation does is lighten your payments (workload) and increase the length of servitude to the lender.

Three Steps toward Freedom from Debt

My personal experience and work with others has led me to identify three steps to freedom from debt. They are:

1. Acquire Knowledge
2. Make Sound Choices
3. Take action

The first step to being free from debt is to acquire something slaves neither have nor believe they can possess: education and knowledge. Read books, listen to CDs, Mp3s, and podcasts or attend seminars. Do something that will increase your financial awareness. If financial matters are not your area of expertise, then hire someone who has the knowledge to help you. Financial loss, which is what debt is, stems from a lack of knowledge. Knowledge enables you to recognize good choices.

Sound choices enable you to decide on a course of action and follow it through to completion. Knowledge and choices work together, because without knowledge you would not be aware of the choices and how to take full advantage of them.

You must make take action to be free (set goals, save, budget, etc.,) because the masters (the person or entity to whom you are in debt) want you to remain in debt so that you can continue to add their wealth. When I started my consulting practice, I applied for and received a credit card, which I used to finance start-up expenses. After I used the card, I always paid five to 10 times more than my minimum monthly payment. After three months, I received an increase to my credit limit. Why did the company give me an increase?

Chapter 5 Your Money is Valuable

They said I was a "good" customer. If I were such a "good" customer, then why not decrease my interest rate, or credit my account?

No, to them a "good" customer was someone who used the card and paid more than the minimum payment. As a result, the company increased my credit limit to encourage me to spend more while maintaining the same payment frequency. The company did not care if I ever paid off the card. Their goal was to use me as a means of cash flow for their business for as long as possible. Hence, they offered me a rock bottom minimum monthly payment with the hope that I would not take action to liquidate my debt.

Without purposeful action, your financial life becomes like that of people who have given up and are praying to win the lottery. There is an answer to your debt problems, but the solution requires action on your part. Without action, we know that your "lip faith" is alive, but your "do faith" is dead. For a financial miracle, it will take some talking (prayer) and some doing (action). What type of action is required? Use the knowledge you have acquired, or the help you have hired, to make sound choices that will take you where you want to go financially. Purposeful action is the vehicle by which we travel to our destination. In this case, the destination is freedom from debt.

Five Steps to Remove Debt

Instead of ignoring or enduring your financial straits you must view your debts with the objective of eliminating as many as possible, as soon as possible.

Make plans, set objectives and goals. Is being debt-free your goal? If so, then you must think about being debt-free every day. Even if you are only able to apply $1 toward your freedom, that's $1 that will bring you closer to your goal of being debt free.

The Growing of You

When freedom became my goal, I started seeing opportunities that I had missed or that I was afraid to attempt. Working to remove debt is an active thought. Active thought is thinking about the solution, not the problem.

What has thinking about debt gotten you? Nothing but worry, anxiety, and fear. In fact, you begin to focus more on the problems, not the solutions which creates a hopeless situation. "Oh poor me, I can't do anything about my debt." Every situation cries out for a solution, but if you are thinking about the problem (being in debt), and not the solution (how to get out of debt), then debt will remain a problem for you.

Debtors who are resigned to remain debtors will be bound their entire lives – even if they experience a financial windfall such as an inheritance or lottery winnings. Debtors who desire to be free from debt, will progress toward being free every day. Using the following steps helped me to rid myself of several thousand dollars of consumer debt.

Make a list of who you owe, include phone numbers, addresses, the amount owed, the monthly minimum payments and interest rate. This gives you the big picture and is a sign of responsibility.

Next, arrange your debts in order from the smallest to largest amount. Prioritize based on your desire to free up as much cash as possible, as soon as possible.

For example, a borrower has three debts:

- $ 750 Balance 19% interest $75 a month payments.
- $ 500 Balance 20% interest $50 a month payments.
- $ 250 Balance 10% interest $25 a month payments.

Some credit counselors would say pay extra money to eliminate the high interest debts first, which is good if saving on interest is your objective. But if you want to prosper and relieve stress, you first need to increase cash flow.

Chapter 5 Your Money is Valuable

Cash flow represents the amount of money flowing into your possession, usually measured on a monthly basis. Paying off the smallest debt first, regardless of interest, increases short-term cash flow and increases your prosperity. Then proceed to the next smallest debt. Remember, the amount of money you free up monthly is the measure of your freedom and ability to prosper.

Set a date by which you want to be free of debt. Be realistic and base your payoff date on your current monthly earnings. When I used this plan, I ended up paying off each debt earlier than I expected. If your present income is not enough, or your credit score is suffering, you may consider reducing your debt by:

a) Contacting creditors and asking for interest rate reduction (thereby decreasing the total amount owed)

b) Use your savings to make a settlement payment offer.

c) Request a temporary reduction in minimum monthly payment.

Lastly, reduce spending by focusing on needs and not wants. I remember years ago living in a tiny studio apartment. My budget was tight, but on Friday nights, I would order a pizza and relax. This happened every Friday. When getting out of debt became my goal, I noticed that I was spending about $10 a week on pizza. That amounted to about $520 a year! Could you imagine? If I continued at that rate for five years, I would spend an amount that would have paid off about one-third of my debts.

What is your spending like? Are you spending money on things that bring short-term satisfaction? Is your spending out of control? Are you acquiring material things that destabilize your financial footing and pull you deeper in debt and away from your financial destination (goals)?

The Lazy Steward became a slave because his state of being was more important than increasing his bag of gold. He was afraid of the Master and decided that in order to feel a sense of peace, he needed to bury his bag of gold. The Lazy Steward was given authority to use the gold, but by not using the money to increase his perception of indebtedness to the Master increased. This eventually led to his bag of gold being given to the Steward with ten bags.

The Parable of the Bags of Gold is filled with symbolism and in this parable there are two forms of debt. The first is consumer debt, which we have covered, and the second is financing debt.

Financing Debt is the use of other people's money (OPM) to increase. Financing debt is future-oriented. The objective of financing debt is to earn money in the future exceeding the amount of money received in the present. In a broad sense, the parable states that the Master gave the stewards bags of gold, which prompted different responses from them. The Good Stewards responded with a sense of gratitude for the benefit of receiving the bags of gold. In gratitude, the Good Stewards were motivated to improve their relationship with the Master that was precipitated by his trust in them.

The Lazy Steward responded with a sense of ingratitude. He viewed the bag of gold as an obligation to repay the Master, and not a benefit, which led to a sense of indebtedness. The feeling of indebtedness motivated the Lazy Steward to respond with fear.

The Good Stewards' prudent use of the gold (financing debt), prospered them and led to an increase and the eventual rule over cities.

To recap, the nature of consumer debt causes one (the lender) to increase and the other (the debtor) to decrease. Remember, money was made to create money, but consumer debt creates money for someone else. The Lazy Steward did not see money as a tool to create more money.

Chapter 5 Your Money is Valuable

Whenever you fail to use money as a means to create money, you lose the ability to view money creatively. Financing debt is the creative use of other people's money (OPM) for an increase. The Good Stewards were given money by the Master, and used the money as a tool to create more money.

To Have and To Share

Giving

Earlier I talked about generosity and how a closed fist cannot receive. By opening your hand to give, you also open it to receive. By giving, you position yourself to receive what you need. You may choose to give to a charitable organization or you may choose to tithe. Those who tithe acknowledge that God owns everything and they honor Him by giving 10% of their income to the poor, churches or other charitable works that serve the greater good. Whether you believe in God or not, tithing benefits the receiver and the giver.

When I moved to my current residence, I was several thousands of dollars in debt. I had no car and no home. Shortly before my arrival in my new city, I adopted the principle of tithing. To say that tithing (along with wise financial planning) contributed greatly to turning my financial picture around would be an understatement. Within three years I received a promotion that more than doubled my income from my previous job. As a result of tithing I was able to pay off all of my debts. I purchased a car, a house and I participated in several investment opportunities. Some call this the law of attraction. By tithing you indicate to God, that you are a trustworthy person willing to work as an agent of abundance to assist those in need. And, as such, you position yourself to receive an abundance to maintain that position.

Saving

Society has conditioned us to ask for and expect instant gratification in all areas of our lives from the food we eat, to the cars we drive. Credit cards give us instant access to items that, we once had to save for. This era of immediacy, and the need to keep up with everyone else, has shifted our focus away from assets (wealth; what a person owns) to creditworthiness (the amount of debt a person can afford). This kind of thinking diminishes the value of saving.

Saving can help you survive and thrive during lean times. Life operates in cycles just like on a farm. There is a time and season for everything, including economies. If you examine the economic history of the nations of the world, you will see that there were times when the economy was robust, and other times when it was a bust. If you desire to be prosperous, you must understand that consistent saving will allow you to prosper during times of abundance and times of famine. Ask any successful farmer about the importance of timing, and he will tell you that timing can mean the difference between prosperity and poverty. When a farmer plants his seed, he does not plant all of them at once. He holds some back because he realizes that replenishment is a key to maintaining a constant flow of fruit.

As you are aware by now, the stewards were similar to our present day money managers. They were given bags of gold to invest in proportion to their abilities. Two were successful, and one was unsuccessful because he did not invest the gold. The curious thing about his actions is that they are contrary to someone who had been trained to manage gold. The Master responds to the Lazy Steward's action by saying, *"Well then, you should have put my money on deposit with the bankers, so that when I returned I would have received it back with interest."*

Are you consistently saving money? Or, are you like the people who, say they can't afford to save now, but will save once they "get rich".

Chapter 5 Your Money is Valuable

They associate saving with being rich, when in reality, saving is a higher thought. This higher thought grants power and the ability to make choices, to meet your goals, and to acquire wealth, something debtors generally believe they are unable to do. Savings will free your mind from focusing exclusively on debt. Like on the farm, you reap what you sow. If you spend more, (you reap the result) you will have less money. If you sow saving, (you will reap the benefit) you have more money.

The most widely accepted amount to save is 10% of your gross (before deductions) or net (take home) pay. The level of saving is based on the individual. Generally, one to three months of your salary is a good goal. There are many who are in such a crisis that they cannot afford to save the full 10%. One simple way to jumpstart your savings plan is to take all the coins that you accumulate in a day and deposit them in a jar or box. Do this each day (be consistent), then at the end of the week, or when the jar is full, take that money to the bank and deposit it into your savings account. This savings technique is a good starting point, because those unaccustomed to savings might get discouraged, if they set their initial goals too high. Establish and maintain the habit. The amount you are able to save may be nowhere near the amount you desire to save, but remember this: there are some tasks that cannot be accomplished immediately and may require time.

Your funds should be placed in a savings vehicle, which is liquid (easily accessible) and that preserves your principal (possesses low risk). Such savings vehicles are Passbook Savings, U.S. Savings Bonds, and Money Market Mutual Funds.

- For a Passbook Savings Account, you take your money to a bank. The bank in turn agrees to hold your money and return a percentage of interest to you.

- U.S. Savings Bonds are products of the government. These are loans you make to "Uncle Sam" guaranteed by the, "full faith and credit of the United States Government."

- A Money Market Mutual Fund or Money Market Fund is simply a portfolio of short-term money market securities that consist of Treasury Bills, commercial paper, etc. They are designed to be extremely safe and conservative.

Saving can also protect you from crises that affect you economically. For example, a spouse may become disabled or die. An event like this can be catastrophic to a family's finances. To lessen the impact of such a catastrophe, I suggest a form of savings called insurance. Insurance protects your family from financial loss due to catastrophic illness, disability or death. In our quest to prosper financially, we tend to overlook the role insurance plays in our personal finances.

Let's say that you are following your financial plan perfectly when your spouse becomes disabled and can no longer work. Suddenly, a source of income that you were depending on is gone. A sudden loss of income can throw the best-laid plans into chaos. Even if you are fortunate enough to have saved for "lean times," your savings is a short-term solution at best. During such unexpected crises, any savings, retirement fund, and investments you may have accumulated are at risk of being consumed to cover expenses.

Insurance protects these resources during a crisis. My insurance agent once told me a story in which he compared insurance to an umbrella that protects your financial lifestyle (savings, home, car, investments, etc.) from the unexpected storms of life (death, hospitalization, disability, etc.). As an "umbrella," insurance provides a measure of protection as you weather those "storms of life".

My "storm of life" came when my wife was unexpectedly diagnosed with a condition, which left her temporarily disabled. After exhausting her paid sick leave, her condition still called for her to take an indefinite unpaid leave of absence from her job. All at once, my wife's salary was removed from our budget.

Chapter 5 Your Money is Valuable

We had savings, investments, and retirement funds that we could tap into, but using those resources would disrupt our financial plan. Fortunately, when we got married my mentor advised me to purchase income and mortgage disability insurance policies. With those policies in place, our financial plan did not suffer because of the missing income. Then after we met certain criteria, the income disability policy provided a pre-arranged, tax-free level of income for a period up to one year, while the mortgage disability policy would pay our mortgage for up to three years. These policies made a potential financial catastrophe into a financially manageable event.

Managing your finances will make unexpected events more manageable. Many people say they want to go to the next financial level, but they continue to operate using the same habits of spending more than they earn, using credit that they cannot afford and refusing to save. Learn to save for what you want and let your finances pull you to your next level.

When I was a teenager I asked my grandfather for a car. He agreed with one stipulation: I had to save for it. So, I began to save diligently and after six months, I had enough money to buy my first car. Purchasing my car, without going into debt planted seeds in me for how to avoid debt in the future. That experience taught me that saving is worth the effort.

It is important to know why you save, as it is to save. Not everyone saves for the right reasons. Greed means to take all you can, with no thought for the needs of others. The nature of greed distorts your view of money and severely limits its flow. Greed leads you to believe that it's more important to hold on to your money. For money to multiply, it must be able to flow freely from you to others; and from others to you. A parable in Luke 12:16-21 (KJV) suggests that greed can kill you.

Greed leads to health problems, which leads to worry and can ultimately lead to death. Stinginess is defined as sharing or spending grudgingly or through necessity only. People who are stingy view savings through the filter of scarcity.

They believe that their savings cannot be replenished and that extreme conservation is a key component to prospering. Savings will enable you to prosper even during lean times. You now control a portion of your finances that debt once controlled. Remember, save for the right reasons and you will see positive results. The increase in the end is greater than in the beginning.

Chapter 6
Increase

Make Sure What Goes Up Stays Up

In the previous chapters, I discussed four financial viewpoints of management (spending, debt, giving, and saving). In addition, there are financial viewpoints of increase (giving, saving, investment, and work). Increase is a mindset; therefore, your mind needs to be conditioned for increase. Four principles for developing a mindset for increase are Diligence, Generosity, Allocation, and Diversification.

- Diligence is defined as work done with careful, steady effort. Diligence allows you to see your success on a daily basis. Diligence begins with a plan for your success and ends with goals being achieved through persistent and consistent effort.

- Generosity is a willingness to give or share unselfishly. The willingness to receive must be met with the willingness to give.

- Allocation, or setting things apart for a specific purpose, is a key to prospering. Allocation of your resources (money, time, and effort) will yield an overall return.

- Diversification means to spread your money across investment opportunities to achieve the delicate balance between risk and return. This principle of investing helps reduce risk and maximize return.

Investment

When the economic cycle is in a state of recession or recovery, perceptive investors look to invest. Remember there is a time and season for everything. Investments should not be viewed as "get rich quick" schemes. They should be viewed for what they are: vehicles for putting money to work to earn a return. While earning high returns are most desirable, it is also important to base investments on your personal investment ability to avoid being caught up in "get rich quick" schemes.

Investing Goals

Your personal goals strongly influence how you choose to invest your money. A good steward will invest and set aside money for his children and for a time when he is physically unable to work.

I have identified four common financial goals:

- Having adequate funds for retirement
- Additional growth asset purchases
- Additional income
- An inheritance

To better help you determine and focus on your personal investment goals, I have included an overview of the four goals cited above.

Retirement Investing

A wise person prepares for his later years by investing financial surplus during his prime work years in order to ensure an adequate standard of living during retirement.

The primary vehicles for retirement investing are:

- 401(k) plans & 403(b) plans
- IRAs

Chapter 6 Increase

- Roth IRAs
- Annuities

401(k) Plans: The 401(k) plans are company-based retirement plans for regular wage earners (receive a W-2 from your employer).

403(b) Plans: The 403(b) plans are tax-exempt company retirement plans. They are similar to 401(k) plans with minor variances: 403(b) plans are not permitted to invest in individual stocks and bonds, and plan participants over age 50 are allowed to contribute additional catch-up amounts.

IRA: Individual Retirement Accounts allow individuals, who may or may not have exceeded their contribution limit on their 401(k) or 403(b), accounts to make individual contributions to their retirement funds. An IRA is similar to 401(k) and 403(b) plans in that the contributions grow tax-deferred and in some cases, IRA contributions are tax-deductible.

Roth IRA: A Roth IRA offers you the ability to make after-tax contributions to your account. If you maintain the account for a minimum of five years and you are at least 59½ years-old, the withdrawals do not have to be included in your gross income for tax purposes. If you meet all the qualifications, then you do not have to pay income tax on this type of account.

Annuities: An annuity allows your money to grow tax-deferred just like 401(k) plans, 403(b) plans and IRAs. Early withdrawals are penalized if taken before age 59½. Annuities are similar to a Roth in that they do not provide any deductible contributions.

There are two major benefits that make annuities attractive to some investors. First, unlike the other retirement vehicles, there is no annual contribution limit. Second, there are no mandatory age withdrawals, so you can leave your money in an annuity for as long as you like. If the annuitant dies before receiving total income payments equal to the purchase price of the annuity, the payments continue to the beneficiary until they equal the purchase price.

Asset/Growth

To properly increase your net worth, you need to manage what you earn now and invest for growth. This type of investing requires patience, because in most cases it takes time for the value of these investments to increase. We learned from the parable of the bags of gold that the Good Stewards took what they had and created growth, increasing both the number and value of their gold. Today, the goal of the Good Steward is to acquire assets that have the potential to increase in value.

The primary vehicles for asset/growth investing are:

- Series EE/I Savings Bonds
- Stocks
- Undeveloped Real Estate

Stocks

Stocks are instruments (or shares) of ownership in companies, and savings bonds are debt instruments of the government. Stock investment requires a certain level of competence to maximize stock earnings.

By utilizing solid management techniques training and financial savvy, investment advisors have greater odds of generating a profit for their clients during a downturn, than most individuals managing their own stocks based on what they learned from a book. Each transaction is an emotional event for the novice investor. On the other hand, a professional stock manager is not emotionally attached to a stock. The manager's objective is to earn a profit for his client. An experienced stock professional knows how to minimize losses and maximize gains. Most novice investors do not possess this skill.

Case in point: Several years ago, when stocks were booming, I received a "tip" from a relative to buy a certain stock. Back then

Chapter 6 Increase

I knew very little about stocks, but based on the "tip", I purchased the stock. Its value increased about 10%. I was ecstatic and wanted to see more. Over the course of two months, that stock took me on an emotional rollercoaster ride because I had a significant amount of money invested. Eventually I arrived at a point where I couldn't take it anymore, and after losing 40% of my original investment value, I sold the stock at a loss. Over the next six months, the value of the stock increased.

So, what's my point? Had I been well versed in stock management (when to buy and sell), perhaps I could have avoided the emotional ups and downs and sold my stock after the original 10% gain. It bears repeating that stock investing can be a challenge to a novice; however, I am aware that some of you may possess the competence to invest in stocks on your own. Still, I take the position of the Master in Matthew 25. He delivered his goods (money) into the hands of his servants. The possession of money didn't make the Master an investment expert. Wise investment strategies require the preservation of capital. The Master realized that someone whose duty it was to increase his investment, would better serve his capital. I would advise you to seek additional guidance before attempting to purchase stock.

Undeveloped Real Estate

Undeveloped Real Estate can also be a tremendous growth asset. In the small town where I grew up, my grandfather and I often traveled to the country store. That "store" was about the size of the average tool shed. When the owner died the property remained vacant for several years. Today if you drive by the site of that old country store, a McDonalds occupies that same space. The property values surrounding the restaurant rose immediately.

My point is this, if you have patience, knowledge, and available cash for real estate taxes and other expenses, you could possibly benefit from purchasing a piece of land that could someday provide a handsome return on your investment.

Inheritance

An inheritance is money, property, or other valuables received by a descendent upon death of the bestower. An inheritance gives your heirs an economic advantage. Consider how your life might have been impacted if you had a financial boost from your grandparents or great-grandparents. Inheritance creates a family legacy.

Buying your children the latest clothes and games offers nothing in comparison to the benefit they would receive from your financial legacy. Sure, it's fine to buy things for your children, but don't go into debt to make those purchases. Don't spend all you have on things that will not outlast the credit card bills. Teaching your children the value of money and how to live within their means is more beneficial to them than you trying to give them everything *you* didn't have growing up.

Ability vs. Risk in Investing

Now that your investment goals have been determined, the next step is to analyze your ability to invest and the risk involved. Ability means skill, expertise, or talent; and risk means the chance of injury or loss. It's my belief that investments should be made based on your own or your investor's ability. The investment climate appears to focus on risk first. Certainly risk is important and should be reviewed with wisdom, but I believe that the parable of the bags of gold gives us insight into how we should invest:

"Again, it will be like a man going on a journey, who called his servants and entrusted his wealth to them. To one he gave five bags of gold, to another two bags, and to another one bag, each according to his ability. (skill in handling money).

The Master is an investor who entrusts his money to those who have skill in investing. A side note in the above passage is the investor's wise use of diversification. Although each servant possessed the ability to provide a return, there was no guaran-

Chapter 6 Increase

tee the servants would produce returns. So, to limit or reduce the risk associated with investing, the investor (Master) diversified the money among his investment team (stewards) to ensure the greatest possible return and smallest risk.

The man who had received five bags of gold went at once, put his money to work, and gained five bags more. So also, the one with two bags of gold gained two more.

The stewards were aware of the risk associated with trading, but their skill at trading greatly increased the likelihood of a return. The steward with one talent was more aware of the risk associated with investing than he was acquainted with his ability. Because of that mindset the steward did not invest and therefore realized no gain. As a result, the investor took back his money and invested with the steward with a proven record of accomplishment. The investor's decision to switch was an astute decision and here's why. He saw that he received an incredible 88% return on his money, as illustrated in the following table.

	Investment	Return	Increase (%)*
Talents	5	5	63.00%
	2	2	25.00%
	1	0	0.00%
Total	8	0	88.00%

*Divide the amount in the return column by total amount originally invested.

Ex. 1) 5 divided by 8 = .63
    2) 2 divided by 8 = .25
    3) 0 divided by 8 = .00

If you had an investment manager with the ability to generate a large return, wouldn't you take money from the underperforming manager and give it to the manager who met or exceeded earning expectations?

Gambling vs. Investing

Remember, gambling, not investing, bears the greatest risk. In gambling you are given odds for winning. With investing your success is determined by your own, or your investment manager's, ability and skills. When it comes to investing, your most important asset isn't necessarily the amount of money you invest, but your knowledge of investments.

Work is More Than Your Job

If you have a job, you earn an hourly wage or a salary in exchange for fulfilling tasks and responsibilities assigned to you by your employer. Most people use the terms *work* and *job* interchangeably, but they fail to understand that work is more than a job. Work is the behavior that contributes to the successful use of your ability on a job. I did not understand this until a lesson from the Parable of the Bags of Gold taught me that employers reward employees, who put their ability to work in order to reach their potential to earn promotions and increases.

"Again, it will be like a man going on a journey, who called his servants and entrusted his wealth to them. To one he gave five bags of gold, to another two bags, and to another one bag, <u>each according to his ability</u>. Then he went on his journey. The man who had received five bags of gold <u>went at once and put his money to work and gained five bags more</u>. So also, the one with two bags of gold gained two more. The man who had received five bags of gold brought the other five. 'Master,' he said, 'you entrusted me with five bags of gold. See, I have gained five more.' "His master replied, 'Well done, good and faithful servant! You have been faithful with a few things; <u>I will put you in charge of many things</u>. Come and share your master's happiness!' "The man with two bags of gold also came. 'Master,' he said, 'you entrusted me with two bags of gold; see, I have gained two more.' "His master replied, 'Well done, good and faithful servant! You have been faithful with a few things; <u>I

Chapter 6 Increase

<u>will put you in charge of many things.</u> Come and share your master's happiness!'

Years ago, I accepted a job that was completely outside my realm of experience. The job duties were so foreign that I considered quitting after one week even though I desperately needed a job. One day during lunch, I shared my feelings with a fellow employee who I befriended. He told me that I would be okay if I simply came to work consistently and on time. If I did that, he said, my employers would teach me the skills I needed for the position. His advice became my mantra, "come to work and be on time". Sure enough, things got better, but I still felt stuck in a rut with no way out. Finally, almost in despair, I decided to stop complaining and do more than simply "come to work and be on time". Although I was not the most skilled employee, I decided to apply my ability to my job. Once I did, an amazing thing happened, my supervisors noticed me and offered me an opportunity to apply for a position that was better suited to my abilities. Within three months, my newfound understanding that *work is more than a job*, led me to use my ability, which led to a promotion and a sizeable salary increase.

Employers are more likely to promote an employee whose ability they see in operation than an employee whose ability, they do not see in operation. Employees who are insubordinate, lack focus, complain, and fail to complete assigned tasks, can be deemed a liability. These behaviors draw your attention away from applying your ability to the job.

Most people who are unaware that they are a liability remain in this state because they find excuses for not using their ability. The irony is that these people see nothing wrong with their behavior and remain convinced they deserve a promotion. The outcome of their behavior is the failure to fulfill their job responsibilities. This disqualifies them from promotion.

"Then the man who had received one bag of gold came. 'Master,' he said, <u>'I knew that you are a hard man, harvesting where you have not sown and gathering where you have not</u>

scattered seed. So I was afraid and went out and hid your gold in the ground. See, here is what belongs to you.' "His master replied, *'You wicked, lazy servant! So you knew that I harvest where I have not sown and gather where I have not scattered seed? Well then, you should have put my money on deposit with the bankers, so that when I returned I would have received it back with interest." 'Take the bag of gold from him and give it to the one who has ten bags. For whoever has will be given more, and they will have an abundance. Whoever does not have, even what they have will be taken from them. And throw that worthless servant outside, into the darkness, where there will be weeping and gnashing of teeth.'*

Are you someone who hides your ability by not applying it to the responsibilities assigned by your employer? Hiding your ability will result in the potential for promotion to remain unrealized. Instead of being a catalyst for promotion, you prove to be a hindrance. The refusal to apply your ability may jeopardize any good standing you have or limit any chance of future advancement. No employer will continue to invest resources in an employee who is not faithfully applying his or her ability to their job. Those rewards will be given to and reinvested in an employee, who faithfully applies his or her ability to reach their potential. Reaching that potential is evidence that employee can handle greater responsibility as a supervisor over more important matters.

"His master replied, 'Well done, good and faithful servant! You have been faithful with a few things; I will put you in charge of many things. Come and share your master's happiness!' "The man with two bags of gold also came. 'Master,' he said, 'you entrusted me with two bags of gold; see, I have gained two more.' "His master replied, 'Well done, good and faithful servant! You have been faithful with a few things; I will put you in charge of many things. Come and share your master's happiness!"

Chapter 6 Increase

When you apply ability to responsibility, you unlock potential. Potential opens an opportunity to use your ability for a higher purpose. My dream is to help people fulfill their purpose, overcome obstacles, enjoy their lives, and contribute to the lives of others. That dream led directly to the creation of this book. Through this book, I've learned that work is more than a job and by taking action to apply my ability reveals potential that will promote me to a higher purpose.

Summary

The four principles for developing a mindset for increase are Diligence, Generosity, Allocation, and Diversification.

- Diligence is defined as work done with careful, steady effort. Diligence allows you to see your success on a daily basis. Diligence begins with a plan for your success and ends with goals being achieved through persistent and consistent effort.

- Generosity is a willingness to give or share unselfishly. The willingness to receive must be met with the willingness to give.

- Allocation, or setting things apart for a specific purpose, is a key to prospering. Allocation of your resources (money, time, and effort) will yield an overall return.

- Diversification means to spread your money across investment opportunities to achieve the delicate balance between risk and return on investment opportunities.

Chapter 7
Management

Mind Over Money

The reason for the financial success of the Good Stewards and the failure of the Lazy Steward comes down to whether or not the stewards knew how to use their bags of gold. In order to use the bags correctly, they needed to understand the power in their hands and respond appropriately. We reap what we sow. This principle is especially true when it comes to how we handle money.

Returning to the farming analogy, the difference in a farmer who prospers and one who struggles, is knowing where to plant. Prosperous farmers will plant seed (money) in good ground (assets) that encourages growth and return. If money is planted in an environment that supports growth, the farmer (investor) can expect a return. Conversely, if money is planted in an environment (bad ground) that is not conducive to growth, the farmer can expect very little return on his seed.

- Money represents seed
- Assets represent good ground
- Income is productive seed that yields fruit
- Liabilities represent bad ground
- Expenses represent unproductive seed that yields no fruit

Chapter 7 Management

Assets: An asset is property that is owned and generates more value or income than it costs to operate or own. There are three types of assets: primary, secondary, and consumable. A clear indication of your financial health is simply where you have planted the majority of your seeds. Each asset brings different financial results when seeds are planted.

Primary assets usually increase in value and have a greater probability of providing a return. The following assets allow money to work for you.

- Cash on hand (Savings Account, Certificate of Deposit (CD), etc.)
- Stock
- Mutual Funds
- Treasury Bills, notes
- Bonds
- Real Estate
- Annuities
- Cash Value of Life Insurance Policies
- Skills/Talents/Abilities

Secondary assets, when properly maintained for a period of time, can potentially generate a return.
- Rare coins
- Stamps
- Other Collectibles

Consumable assets are temporary assets whose value tends to decrease (depreciate) over the life of the asset. Consumable assets can still create income; however, money generated from their sale often will not exceed the original purchase price. Personal property (cars, boats, furniture, etc.,) is listed as a consumable asset because it loses value soon after being purchased. The process is depreciation. Depreciation is a decrease in value of property through wear, deterioration, or obsolescence.

- Cell Phone
- Television
- Clothes
- Car
- Furniture
- Computer

Understanding the differences between each asset is crucial. Where is your money planted? People who plant their money in consumable assets appear to be wealthy and prosperous, but only for a season. Once consumable assets lose their usefulness the loss in value follows. The nature of secondary assets is that their value is based on their rarity, which means that they require time to increase in value. Only primary assets offer a consistent means for generating increase.

Income

Income is the fruit that results from planting seed in good ground. If money is seed and assets are good ground, then what do you reap from sowing seeds in good ground? The answer is income. Income is money or value realized from investments, work, or services and products. In other words, income grows from assets. There are three types of income: passive, earned, and service/product:

- Passive Income is received from non-active investing

- Earned Income is received from employment in a business

- Service/Product income is received from providing a service or product to customers

A prosperous farmer uses money (seeds) to purchase and maintain primary assets in excess of his expenses. By planting his money in those assets, he generates a return. A poor farmer spends more than he has to purchase consumable and secondary assets. This process creates liabilities, increases expenses and eventually causes a financial decrease.

Liabilities

Bad ground has weeds and thorns; and weeds choke seed. If money represents seeds, then there are places you can plant your money that will choke it and prevent it from growing. Liabilities represent bad ground. To put it simply, liabilities are debt. By generating liabilities, you are planting your money in ground filled with weeds that choke the life out of seed and prevent it from growing.

Examples of liabilities include mortgages, personal loans, credit card debt, auto loans, school loans, etc.

- Liabilities grow when you purchase things you cannot afford on credit instead of using cash.

- Liabilities grow when money is spent on things that do not grow in value.

Purchases on Credit: Let's say that you are shopping and you see an outfit that you *must* have, but you do not have the money for the outfit. What you do have is your credit card, so you whip it out and charge it! Congratulations, you just increased your liabilities: the use of credit to purchase non-income producing items.

Items That Don't Grow in Value: Everything purchased is either an asset or a liability. By purchasing things that don't grow in value, you increase your liabilities. Even something with great sentimental value, like an engagement ring, or car, will not help you reach your financial goals. The more liabilities you have, the less likely you are to turn your seed into fruit; instead you will choke your money.

The following are examples of liabilities:

- House Mortgage
- Car/Auto/Consumer/School Loan
- Credit Card

Some of you might challenge the listing of a mortgage as a liability, but if you have a mortgage, you don't own the house, the bank does. The banks provide the opportunity of home ownership, and they charge you for that opportunity. The charge is the interest you pay in addition to the principal (or loan amount). Once you repay the loan with interest, you own the house.

Expenses

Expenses are items charged against income and that cause an outflow of cash. Expenses consume income and reduce net income. They subtract your fruit. Expenses include utilities, taxes, entertainment, food, clothes, auto loan payments, mortgage payments, credit card payments, etc. Expenses are a part of life; however, you must be careful not to allow expenses to grow and consume more of your income than is necessary.

If you work and are only making enough to survive, then you must change how you plant seed. If you continue with the status quo, the only people who will benefit from your work will be your employer, the government, and your creditors. Individuals with low or high incomes can be affected by this condition. If your income is substantial, yet you find yourself close to losing your home, car, or if you are being threatened with utility disconnections, or are being hounded by bill collectors, you must change your mindset. If you don't, it will be harder for you to finance your dreams and goals, which will be a greater loss.

Balance Sheet: The balance sheet shows your total assets, liabilities, and net worth. Take a sheet of paper and divide it into two columns. The total sum value of your assets is placed on the left side, and your liabilities are listed on the right. Net worth is what is left after figuring total assets minus total liabilities.

Chapter 7 Management

(+1,500) Assets (-1,000) Liabilities (=500) Total Net Worth

Type	Assets (+)	Liabilities (-)	Net Worth (=)
Stocks	500		
Savings	1,000		
Credit Card		1,000	
Net Worth (=)			500

These figures can have a direct effect on your income statement. Assets increase income, while liabilities increase expenses. Which do you have more of: assets or liabilities? If you answered assets, then what type of assets do you have? Most people have consumable assets. Consumable assets are the least beneficial because they depreciate (lose value). In addition, liabilities (debt) are often incurred to acquire them and those liabilities generate expenses.

Income Statement Your income and expenses are part of an income statement. To determine your monthly income, divide a sheet of paper into halves. The top half is for income and the bottom half is for expenses. If your total monthly income is greater than your total monthly expenses, then there is a net income. If your total expenses are greater than your total income, then there is a net loss.

(+) Income (-) Expenses (=) Equals Net Income (+) or Loss (-)

Type	Income (+)
Salary	2,000
Interest Income	10
TOTAL INCOME	2,010
Type	Expense (-)
Rent	900
Loan Payment	500
Utilities	400
TOTAL EXPENSES	1,800
Net Income (+) or Loss (-)	**210**

The Growing of You

Congratulations! You have created a financial statement. Now, how do you determine if you are progressing financially, or if you need to make some changes? Financial ratios measure how well you handle your money based on the information you listed on your financial statements. I will discuss these four ratios: Solvency, Liquidity, Savings, and Debt Service.

Solvency Ratio
Total assets ÷ Total debts = Solvency Ratio

This ratio determines the extent to which the value of your existing assets (if sold) would be enough to pay off your total debts. Your ability to satisfy your debts with your existing assets is solvency. A good solvency ratio is when your assets (i.e., stocks, bonds, and home value, etc.), equal or exceed your liabilities (i.e., school loan, mortgage, credit cards, etc.) by 1.5 or greater.

Let's look at the solvency ratios of two couples.

Couple A has $50,000 in assets and $10,000 in debt. Their Solvency Ratio is: 5.00

Total Assets (divided by) Total Debts = Ratio
$50,000 (÷) $10,000 = 5.00

This couple's assets are valued at five times the amount of their debt. They are extremely solvent as their excellent ratio indicates.

The same can't be said for this next couple.

Couple B has $10,000 in assets and $50,000 in debt. Their Solvency Ratio is 0.20.

Total Assets (divided by) Total Debts = Ratio
$10,000 ÷ $50,000 = 0.20

Chapter 7 Management

This couple is insolvent. If their creditors were to call for immediate payment of all their debt, they would not have sufficient assets for repayment. Even after selling everything they own, they could only repay 20% of their debts.

A ratio less than 1.5 can be an indication of problems.

Liquidity Ratio
Liquid Assets ÷ Monthly Expenses = Ratio
This ratio determines the extent to which your current liquid assets (cash and cash equivalents) would be able to satisfy your total monthly expenses, in the event your monthly income was interrupted.

Using the following information on couple A, we can calculate their Liquidity Ratio.

LIQUID ASSETS
Cash on hand: $1,000
Savings Account: $2,000
Money Market: $2,000
EXPENSES
Utilities: $1,000
Mortgage: $1,000
Car Payment: $700

Liquid Assets ÷ Monthly Expenses = Liquidity Ratio
$5,000 (÷) $2,700 = 1.85

In the event of a loss of income, couple A would be able to pay their monthly expenses for only about two months. Conventional financial planning calls for a minimum ratio of 3 or higher.

Savings Ratio
Annual Savings ÷ Gross Income = Savings Ratio
This ratio determines the extent to which you save a portion of your income.

Conventional financial planning calls for a savings ratio range of 8% to 20%. Reaching this savings ratio range consistently provides a surplus that can be used for investment alternatives with a higher investment entry point.

Let's take another example. Couple Y has $800 in annual savings and earn an annual gross income of $40,000. Their Savings Ratio is:

Total Annual Savings (÷) Total Gross Income = Income Ratio
$800 ÷ $40,000 = 0.02

This couple's savings represent only 2% of their gross income. They are not saving enough money of their gross income. A ratio that is .08 or greater indicates a healthy rate of savings. A ratio less than .08 can be an indication of potential financial problems.

Debt Service Ratio
Total Monthly Loan Payments ÷ Monthly Gross Income = Debt Service Ratio

This ratio determines what percentage of your income is spent each month on debt repayment (percentage of your monthly income that is planted in bad ground). The greater the percentage spent on debt repayment, the less there is for savings, investing, and giving. Using the following information, we can calculate the debt service ratio for couple Y.

Mortgage: $1,000; Car Payment: $700
Total Loan Payments = $1,700

Annual Income: $40,000 ÷ 12 months = $3,333.33

Total Monthly Loan Payments ÷ Monthly Gross Income = Debt Service Ratio
$1,700 ÷ $3,333.33 = .51 or 51%

Chapter 7 Management

Couple Y spends approximately 51% of their gross monthly income on debt repayments. This falls outside of the acceptable range of 0% to 37%. Because this couple's debt service ratio exceeds 37%, they need to concentrate their efforts on debt reduction.

Some of you might be wondering why these ratios are so important to your financial profile. Let me share a story on why these ratios are important to your financial health.

A client (I'll call her Laura) and I set out to create her financial statements. Laura focused on the income statements, because she had a financial surplus. Laura thought she was doing fine financially because she had enough money to pay her monthly debts, but she had not considered the financial ratios.

The first ratio I calculated was her savings ratio. Her savings ratio revealed that on an annual basis she saved less than 1% of her annual gross salary. This indicated that, although she could afford to pay her debt (the major concern of most people), she did not pay herself an adequate wage (savings). She spent 99% of her annual gross income, which means <u>99% of *her* money was going into the hands of other people</u>.

Here's another way to look at this startling revelation. If Laura earns $20,000 annually and continues to work for 30 years with no change in salary, then after 30 years she will earn a gross income total of $600,000 (20 x $30,000). Let's also say that Laura doesn't change her savings habits over this period. If she consistently saves 1% of her annual gross salary (excluding interest, she will only have $6,000 in savings. Multiply her annual salary by her annual savings rate ($20,000 x .01) equals annual savings. Then multiply this figure (200) by 30 years to arrive at $6,000. How would you feel if after 30 years of hard work you saved only $6,000?

Had Laura saved 10% of her annual income, she would have $60,000 excluding any potential interest earned from investments, which would result in an even greater return.

The Growing of You

As you can imagine, she was shocked that her lack of savings would have such an impact on her future.

The chart below provides examples of the impact of saving 1% versus 10% of your salary annually and over 30 years.

Annual Salary	Annual 1% Savings	30-Year Projection 1% Annual Savings	Annual 10% Savings	30-Year Projection 10% Annual Savings
30,000	300	9,000	3,000	90,000
40,000	400	12,000	4,000	120,000
50,000	500	15,000	5,000	150,000
75,000	750	22,500	7,500	225,000
100,000	1,000	30,000	10,000	300,000

If you find yourself in a situation where your finances are out of balance, here are some actions that will improve your balance.

1. Tithe (10% of your earnings to your house of worship)
2. Save (a portion of income for yourself)
3. Give (to ministries and charities)
4. Invest (put your money to work for you)
5. Reduce liabilities (review living expenses)

The reduction of liabilities also causes a reduction in expenses once the debt is paid. This improves your balance because once your liabilities decrease, your assets increase in relation to your net worth and provide additional income. Finally, you must work on improving your ability to generate finances. Remember the Parable of the Bags of gold. Each steward received money (bags of gold) according to his ability. Keep this in mind: you can improve your position by perfecting your abilities, thereby increasing the amount of money you receive.

Chapter 7 Management

Summary

Prosperous farmers will plant seed in good ground that encourages growth and return.

If seed is planted in an environment that supports growth, the farmer can expect a ground that is not conducive to growth, the farmer can expect very little return on his seed.

If we view our money as seed and our actions with our money comparable to the actions of a farmer with his seed, then a fairly clear picture of how money grows can be seen.

- Money represents seed
- Assets represent good ground
- Income is productive seed that yields fruit
- Liabilities represent bad ground
- Expenses represent unproductive seed that yields no fruit

Assets: An asset is property that is owned and generates more value or income than it costs to operate or own.

Income: Income is the fruit that results from planting seed in good ground.

Liabilities represent bad ground. Liabilities are debt.

Expenses are items charged against income and that cause an outflow of cash. Expenses are unproductive seed that yield no fruit which forces the farmer to subtract from his existing fruit.

The farming process is tracked using financial statements. The Balance Sheet tracks the amount of seed (money) that you planted in both good ground (assets) and bad ground (liabilities). An Income Statement tracks the seeds that produced fruit (income that you have earned), and seed that did not produce fruit (expenses that you spent).

Chapter 8
Money Perceived is Money Received

Walking the Budget Tightrope

The establishment and maintenance of a budget is a key component to managing your funds. Budgeting is more than simply recording your income and expenses. A budget serves a twofold purpose: It determines your goal line and how you will get there. The establishment and maintenance of your budget requires three essential components: time, attention, and effort.

Time

Time used wisely is one important factor of successful people. Who among us has become a champion athlete, an accomplished speaker, or received some level of success, without the wise use of time?

If you are not as successful as you would like to be, then examine how you use your time. There is a relationship between time and money. It takes time to understand your budget, to create financial statements, to review and compare data, and to complete activities essential to your management balance. The amount of time used for this purpose reflects your financial management balance. Remember, you reap what you sow. If you use (sow) time wisely in money management, you will reap the benefits of managed money.

Attention

With all things considered, what's the difference in the Good Stewards and the Lazy Steward? The Good Stewards focused their attention on investing their bags of gold, but the Lazy Steward focused his attention on hiding his bag of gold.

Chapter 8 Money Perceived is Money Received

In Chapter 2, I shared how divided attentions can hinder your success. Humans have a limited ability to pay attention to the world around them. Whatever you pay attention to becomes real to you, and what you don't pay attention to is ignored. Therefore, if you don't pay attention to budgeting, it will be easy to spend more than you earn, accumulate consumer debt, and ignore the signs of financial disaster, because the limits of your money are not real to you. If you pay attention to your budget and its relationship to your income and expenses, solutions to your financial problems will become reality to you.

Effort

Finally, with time and attention already devoted toward budgeting, the final piece needed to create and maintain a budget is effort. I'm sure there are some of you who may have tried to set up a budget, but failed to maintain it beyond a short period of time. Without a commitment to effort, it becomes easier to say that you are aware of your financial difficulties, know that you need to budget, but decide that budgeting won't work for you. You are correct, a budget won't work for you, because you must work on it. Sustained effort toward budgeting is needed to understand how you view money and the most appropriate way for you to manage it.

The Money You See Is The Money You Get

- A Consumer is someone who consumes (economic) goods.

- A Provider is someone who supplies (economic) goods for sustenance or support.

- A Producer is someone who produces (economic) goods.

In Chapter 3, I shared a story about two shoe salesmen, who had wildly different results. The first salesman, after seeing that none of the villagers wore shoes concluded that it would be *impossible* to sell shoes to the villagers.

The second salesman, after seeing that none of the villagers wore shoes, concluded that it would be *impossible not* to sell the villagers shoes. Perception played a large part in the success and failure of each salesman. To reinforce this point in the Parable of the Bags of Gold each steward:

- Received the bags of gold from the Master
- Received the bags of gold according to their abilities
- Received the bags of gold at the same time
- Received the bags of gold during the same environmental condition

While the Good Stewards were successful, the Lazy Steward was not. All things being equal, the one factor that contributed to their success or failure was perception. Each steward's perception was the impetus for the action he took with his money.

The Good Stewards perceived

1. The Master as an investor
2. The bags of gold as an investment opportunity

The Lazy Steward perceived

1. The Master as a hard man
2. The bag of gold as a burden

Each of us views finances through one or more financial viewpoints. By viewpoints, I mean a person's perception about money and how it prompts him to use his money.

For example, let's say you found $100 on a sidewalk. If you are a consumer, your first thought would be to buy something or pay a bill. A provider, however, might save the money or give a portion of it to someone in need. A producer would use the $100 to accumulate more money.

Chapter 8 Money Perceived is Money Received

When your focus is limited to your main viewpoint, it becomes your financial weakness. A miser is someone whose saving habits are extreme and rigid. Because he has no concept of the producer viewpoint, he believes that his money is for hoarding. A miser does not see his seed as a resource for investing.

To prosper, you must remember that you reap what you sow: if you sow money consistently using the correct viewpoint at the right time then you will reap the fruit of that viewpoint.

Consumer Viewpoint

The Consumer Viewpoint consists of spending and debt. Spending includes money you spend on yourself or others. For example, this would include money spent on entertainment, jewelry, and clothes. Debt is money spent on obligations.

Spenders

A Spender views cash as means to acquire material things. If cash is unavailable, extreme spenders will use a credit card to make an unaffordable purchase. Spenders fail to see the value of investing, saving, and in helping others. Spenders want whatever they want, and the impact on their finances is not their main concern until they find themselves unable to spend more or in debt.

Debtor

A debtor is a consumer who sowed excessive spending and reaped the fruit of debt. His limited perception to the consumer viewpoint undermines his attempts to get out of debt, and in fact creates more debt. I know a debtor who created more debt through several bad financial decisions like borrowing money from others, and writing overdraft checks to cover expenses until she could borrow more money. A debtor's mindset circumvents any opportunities to save, give, invest or achieve personal goals. Debtors are only concerned with reducing their debt obligations to spend.

The Growing of You

These obligations originate through:

1. Overspending
2. Under-earning
3. Lack of planning

As mentioned earlier, excessive spenders spend beyond their resources and create debt. Overspending, without regard to managing or creating money, leads to debt. Excessive spenders believe in treating themselves to extravagances because they have worked hard to pay their bills and obligations. These extravagances may not be luxurious, but wasteful spending based on desire without any thought for need or affordability.

Under-earners are not usually "big spenders." They simply lack the money necessary to meet their needs. This mindset arises when an under-earner is not adequately compensated for his or her talent. Not knowing your worth can lead to a loss of income or even a devaluation of your talents. Under-earners are often targets for unscrupulous lenders who make loans with huge interest rates or offer credit limits that put the under-earner deeper in debt.

Spenders who earn enough money for their needs, but who often find themselves in debt are known as marginal spenders. The reason they are in debt is because of a lack of planning. Any unexpected event (home or car repairs, medical occurrence, a temporary work stoppage, etc.) can cause their finances to hit a tailspin. Of course, while all of this is happening, their obligations continue to mount. Without prior planning for these "unforeseen events of life" through insurance and/or savings, maintaining their current standard of living can be difficult at best.

Some people have what I refer to as tunnel vision. They fail to see the potential for life's twists and turns. Another example might be a former client of mine who had no plan for a loss of job, loss of spouse, or any event of life; he simply expected his financial outlook to remain the same.

Chapter 8 Money Perceived is Money Received

Provider Viewpoint

A provider seeks to provide for himself (saving) and, or others (giving). Saving is an outflow from your budget and is not a detractor. The act of saving adds to your overall bottom line. Saving is an essential part of any spending plan. By managing your money to provide for saving and giving, you gradually expand your consumer viewpoint to include the provider viewpoint. As you save for yourself, and give a portion to others, more is given to you so that you may have an abundance of money. Opening your hand to give also opens it to receive what you need.

Producer Viewpoint

A producer seeks to benefit the world (his surroundings) by what he does. He is extremely focused on increasing. Producers will work long hours to increase financially. Producers are driven to do more than the status quo. Because of their extreme ability to produce, producers can suffer from lack of financial management.

I once served as a consultant for a producer who had lax money management skills. His inability to manage money was the culprit behind his inability to properly benefit from his labors. He complained of experiencing "burnout" and uneasy feelings of never having enough money. Another way to view producers is that they are so focused on producing, that they are unaware of what their money has already produced. This viewpoint contributes to "burnout" and is a factor in producing shorter life spans for men. There are other producers who have increased exponentially and they don't know what to do with their money.

There are producers who have adopted a balanced viewpoint by expanding their viewpoint to include providing. Bill Gates is a producer who believes he can most benefit the world by what he does, which is to help computer users all over the world. His status as one of the richest men in the world is a byproduct of his beliefs.

The Growing of You

As a result of his viewpoint, Mr. Gates has contributed hundreds of millions of dollars through his foundation and other philanthropic endeavors.

Conflict of Viewpoints

No two people view money exactly the same, and at no time are those points of view more evident than during marriage. This explains why the greatest threat to most relationships involves money. Prior to the marriage, each partner handled money according to one, possibly two, of the aforementioned financial viewpoints. So, when a couple marries and they are confronted with financial viewpoints different from what they are used to, conflict can erupt. What marriage wouldn't experience conflict when one spouse's financial viewpoint is to work, work, and work some more for money, while the other spouse's financial viewpoint is to spend, spend, and spend some more. Eventually something will break, and usually it's one spouse's patience. Another example of an opposing viewpoint is when one spouse would "give the shirt off of his/her back" to help someone in need, while the other spouse who has reservations about giving to others *before* family obligations are met.

At the core, there is nothing inherently wrong with any of the three (consumer, provider, producer) viewpoints. Problems arise when you embrace a myopic focus on your primary money viewpoint, regardless of the situation. For example, those who have an extreme viewpoint of production may appear to be workaholics or greedy. Those who focus only on consumption may experience poverty or incessant indebtedness. Those who focus only on providing may become miserly or irresponsible.

Balanced Viewpoint

What is your first memory of money? Were you taught that money should be spent as soon as you got it, or did you learn that you must work or use your wits to acquire your desires? Our views on money develop during childhood. I know people who use post-dated checks as a way to cover expenses.

Chapter 8 Money Perceived is Money Received

Unfortunately, these parents are unknowingly teaching their children to adopt this habit once they become adults. This cycle can stop with you. When your children receive money, ask them what they want to do with the money. The answer will give you an indication of what he/she has learned from you.

The goal of the Stewardship Model is to blend all viewpoints to eliminate the potential danger of operating solely in an individual viewpoint. A balanced money viewpoint enhances the effectiveness of your primary viewpoint. For example, a consumer who understands the importance of expanding his awareness to include provider and producer viewpoint, will have more money to spend, will be a savvy consumer, and will be less likely to get in debt. A balanced viewpoint emancipates you from the spending/debt-paying cycle, because you will regain control of your money. As I mentioned earlier, producers increase to the extent they are not aware of how effectively their money works for them. Producers who have a balanced viewpoint will acquire a purpose for their efforts: savings for themselves, giving to others, and permitting themselves to spend some of the money. Once this balance is achieved, burnout ends and the producer gains a renewed focus. It is important to remember that there is a time to consume, a time to produce, and a time to provide.

The way we handle our finances should be a reflection of all three viewpoints. A balanced money philosophy is the foundation upon which Financial Stewardship operates.

Financial Management and Your Viewpoint

Identifying your viewpoint is the first step in proper money management. It helps you discover the cause of potential problems that extend beyond having more expenses than income.

A spending plan or a budget contains techniques that help you manage money, while your money viewpoint is your approach to handling money. We tend to see the world in shades of black, white, or gray, and we act accordingly.

Financial viewpoints influence how you manage your money. Managing money with a generalized spending plan or a budget places the onus on the person who has discipline to spend less than he or she earns. But this approach doesn't work for people who lack discipline to spend less than they earn. It does not take their financial viewpoints into consideration. Personalizing your budget becomes easier because it takes your financial viewpoint into consideration.

For example, let's say that my fictional spender is named Diana. Her income is sufficient to meet her needs, but she shops almost non-stop. Diana has a consumer viewpoint. She likes to spend money, but she doesn't budget for her expenses, therefore she gets depressed because she lacks discipline. If Diana can change her habit, by allocating a portion of her money for the things she likes, she can align her budget with the way she views money.

Getting Started

In order to create a budget that takes your financial viewpoint into account, determine the Average Propensity. The Average Propensity is calculated by taking the percentage of your total dollars used for spending, giving, debt paying, savings and investing.

Debt Paying: Needs such as mortgage, car payment, utilities, rent, and gas. Obligations such as credit cards

Spending: Wants such as gadgets, vacations, eating out

Savings: Money set aside for reserves and emergencies

Investing: Money set aside for growth and increase.

For the sake of this example let's say that out of your total income of $10, you have a total of $7 devoted to debt payouts, $.50 towards spending, $1 devoted to giving, $1 allocated to savings and $.50 towards investing.

Chapter 8 Money Perceived is Money Received

The following chart provides an example of the allocation of your income.

	Consumer	Provider	Producer
Spending	$.50		
Debt-Paying	$7		
Giving		$1	
Savings		$1	
Investing			$.50

Review your finances and record the amount spent for each category. Then, divide each amount by the sum of your finances to arrive at your ratio. For example, let's say your monthly income is $10. The following is how you reported your breakdown: spending 50 cents; debt $7; saving $1; giving $1; and investing 50 cents. Your money management chart would look like this:

	Consumer	Provider	Producer
Spending	5% or .5/10		
Debt-Paying	70% or 7/10		
Giving		10% or 1/10	
Savings		10% or 1/10	
Investing			5% or .5/10

The destination (minimum standard) one should strive for is 75% consumer side, 20% provider side and 5% producer side. The following chart provides an example of the ratio.

	Consumer	Provider	Producer
Spending	5%		
Debt-Paying	70%		
Giving		10%	
Savings		10%	
Investing			5%

The Growing of You

Review Here's another example, let's say your monthly income is $10. The following is how you reported your breakdown: spending $2; debt $7; saving 50 cent; giving 50 cent. Your money management chart would look like this:

	Consumer	Provider	Producer
Spending	20% or 2/10		
Debt-Paying	70% or 7/10		
Giving		5% or .50/10	
Savings		5% or .50/10	
Investing			0%

Based on the results of the ratio, this individual spends a whopping 20% of his inflow on himself and 70% of his inflow on debt. The excessively high spending ratio contributes to the high-debt paying ratio. This person saves and gives, but not enough to become an effective provider. In addition, he fails to set aside money for investing. This person should do one of the following: reduce spending, reduce debt payments, or reduce both categories to allocate more for providing, and producing.

Special Note: People have asked me why they seem unable to make ends meet even though they have sufficient earnings. The answer is their thought patterns need to broaden. If your financial viewpoints remain unchanged, you cannot perceive an increase. You will create an inability to make ends meet no matter your earnings.

I have learned that the less money spent on consumption and debt payment -- without sacrificing shelter, food, clothing, and other necessities -- the more is available for saving, giving and investing. I strive to spend money efficiently on the consumption/debt paying side, so that I can increase money "deposited" on the giving/saving side.

Chapter 9
The Stewardship Model

The End is The Beginning

We have covered the three aspects of stewardship: Time Stewardship, Personal Stewardship and Financial Stewardship. Today, you were introduced to secrets that have been developed into my revolutionary four-step process called the Stewardship Model.

Time Stewardship:
    Acknowledge: There are 24 hours in a day
    Accept Responsibility: To get things done
    Affirm: To work efficiently
    Act: Treat each day as if it were your last

Personal Stewardship:
    Acknowledge: The power of your gift
    Accept responsibility: To fulfill your purpose
    Affirm: To develop your potential
    Act: To describe and deliver your gift, connecting with the world

Financial Stewardship
    Acknowledge: Money is not yours
    Accept responsibility: To manage it
    Affirm: To increase it
    Act: To enjoy your prosperity and share it with the world

As with any story, there is always a greater meaning than what is viewed at face value. The greater meaning of the Parable of the Bags of Gold is located within the characters and symbols themselves.

The Master represents God. God gives us gifts, according to our ability, as a sign of His goodness. The gifts reveal his character to us. He believes that we have the ability to do great things, and that he can trust us to manage and increase His gifts. Most people don't see the true character of God, even though He has freely given us His gifts for a lifetime. Some people get angry with God, because they perceive Him incorrectly and respond according to their perception, and not according to His goodness and character. The Master equipped you with the tools you need to prosper. Your gifts enable you to get wealth.

The Good Stewards represent people who manage their abilities and talents and thereby increase. They understand that the bags of gold represent God's goodness. They make an effort to share the goodness of God with others. As they use their gifts to share the goodness of God, the value of those gifts increase.

The Lazy Steward represents people who do not manage or increase. The Lazy Steward does not see the gift of God as a sign of His goodness. The Lazy Steward has an inaccurate perception of God, which results in a negative emotional response to God's goodness. Instead of being drawn to God, the Lazy Steward reacts with fear and runs away from God: he hides his gifts from himself and from others.

It's my firm belief that the parable is an example of how God views us and how we should view God. The way to accurately view God begins with repentance (changing your mind) from a misconception that He is not good or that He is angry with you. He wants you to see the truth, even if it takes your entire life. He loves you and he gave Himself for you. However, some people never see the truth of God. In order to see the truth of God, repentance is required.

Take time to see the goodness of God in your life. I know that your life is not perfect, and He never promised that it would be. We live in an imperfect world that is sustained by a perfect God. The key to receiving everything that God has for you is to acknowledge him as God, accept His gifts and use them.

Chapter 9 The Stewardship Model

Our success or lack of success is based on our accurate view of God and the faithful use of our gifts as a guide to what life will be like in Heaven. The kingdom of Heaven includes redeemed people who believed God, and use their gifts for good stewardship.

Are you in need of redemption? Redemption (salvation) is available by confessing with your mouth and believing with your heart that Jesus is the Son of the Living God and that God raised Him from the dead. *For with the heart one believes to righteousness, and with the mouth, confession is made to salvation.* (Romans 10:10)

If you have chosen to partake in this free offer, please say this earnest prayer to God: Lord, I admit that I am a sinner. I am sorry for all the sins I have committed against you and others. Please forgive me. I accept your forgiveness and believe that You (Jesus) are the Son of the Living God, and that you died for my sins past, present, and future. I believe that you arose from the dead. I ask that you come into my life as my Savior.

If you sincerely prayed that simple, but powerful prayer, you can rest assured that you received the gift of eternal life and have been forgiven of all your past, present, and future sins. Believe God, seek out a bible-based church, and embark on your new life in God by studying the Bible. I recommend starting in the Book of John. His book was written from a viewpoint that helps readers believe in God.

In closing, I sincerely hope this book has been a blessing to you, as it has been to me to write.

I pray that God will prosper you in all things and that you will be in health, just as your soul prospers. (3 John 2.)

If you are interested in having Michael D. Fluker conduct a seminar, conference, or retreat with your organization, please contact:

Rhapsody Publications
P.O. Box 991
Tallevast, FL 34270
941-866-1955

Or visit

www.rhapsodypublications.net

for more information

Chapter 9 The Stewardship Model

www.ingramcontent.com/pod-product-compliance
Lightning Source LLC
Chambersburg PA
CBHW071708090426
42738CB00009B/1704